Exploring SciTech English

KAIRYUDO

CONTENTS

4　**UNIT 1** 難易度 ★　**Fly Your Plane**

12　**UNIT 2** 難易度 ★★　**The History of QR Code**

18　Basic Terms for Science: Mathematics 1
19　Basic Terms for Science: Mathematics 2

20　**UNIT 3** 難易度 ★★　**Codes and Ciphers**

28　**UNIT 4** 難易度 ★★　**Can Robots Be Good Companions?**

Science Lab

36　1　Magnus Effect
38　2　Supercooling
40　Lab Report

42　Basic Terms for Science: Mathematics 3
43　Basic Terms for Science: Chemistry

| 44 | **UNIT 5** 難易度 ★★★☆ **Laterality:** Left-handed versus Right-handed |

| 52 | **UNIT 6** 難易度 ★★★☆ **The *Challenger* Disaster:** Why Did It Happen? |

- 61 Column: Decision Making
- 64 Basic Terms for Science: Physics 1
- 65 Basic Terms for Science: Physics 2

| 66 | **UNIT 7** 難易度 ★★★ **Lucky Number 113** |

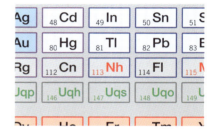

- 74 理系論文を読むために：1　ディスコースマーカー

Science Lab

- 76 **3 Gyro Effect**
- 78 **4 Vibration Control Structure**
- 80 Presentation

- 82 理系論文を読むために：2　統計の読み取り方

| 84 | **UNIT 8** 難易度 ★★★★ **Truth, Beauty, and Other Scientific Misconceptions** |

- 92 Expand Your Vocabulary

ダウンロード方法については，
p.11をご参照ください。

音声ダウンロード用QRコード ▶

UNIT 1 Fly Your Plane

When birds and aircraft fly, moving air around their wings helps carry them high into the sky. Building and flying a model plane will help show you how moving air lifts up a wing and keeps it airborne.

Pre-Reading Activity

Tape cotton threads to two lightweight balls and hang them about 15 cm apart. Try blowing air through the space between the balls. Describe what happens.

Words & Phrases
- aircraft [éərkræft]
- lightweight [láitwèit]
- describe [diskráib]
1. dart [dɑːrt]
3. instruction [instrʌ́kʃən]
3. experiment [ikspérəmənt]
5. findings [fáindiŋz]
6. adjustment [ədʒʌ́stmənt]
10. flap [flæp]

Fold a sheet of paper to make a simple paper dart or model plane. If you don't know how to do this, ask an adult or look on the Internet for folding instructions. Experiment with throwing your plane and see how it flies.

Record your findings.

Now make adjustments to its shape and balance to see how these affect the way it flies. Start by bending up the back edge of both wings. What effect does this have? Now bend up the back of just one wing. Does it still fly straight? What happens if you bend one flap or both flaps downward?

Fly Your Plane

To change the balance of the plane, attach a paper clip to the front of it. How does this affect the flight pattern? Attach the paper clip to the tail of the plane instead and see what difference this makes. Can you make your plane loop the loop or fly in a circle?

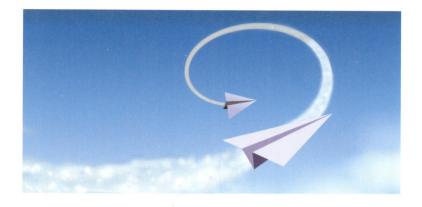

p.4
Words & Phrases

10. **downward**
    [dáunwərd]

Notes

airborne
[éərbɔ̀ːrn]
(陸を離れて)空中にいること

p.5
Words & Phrases

1. **attach**
   [ətǽtʃ]
1. **clip**
   [klip]
4. **loop**
   [luːp]

Notes

4. **loop the loop**
   宙返りをする

Post-Reading Activity

1. If you don't know how to make a model plane, what should you do?

_____

_____

2. Why did you make adjustments to the plane's shape?

_____

_____

3. Why did you attach a paper clip to the front of the plane?

_____

_____

_____

UNIT 1

Pre-Reading Activity

What forces do you think planes need to fly themselves? List them and discuss this topic with your fellow students.

Words & Phrases
4. **glider**
   [gláidər]
6. **propeller**
   [prəpélər]
8. **upward**
   [ápwərd]
11. **disadvantage**
   [dìsədvǽntidʒ]

Notes
1. **gravity**
   [grǽvəti]
   重力
3. **thrust**
   [θrʌst]
   推進力
8. **lift**
   [lift]
揚力
10. **drag**
   [dræg]
   抗力

Gravity is the force that acts on all objects and pulls them toward the center of the Earth. The greater the mass of an airplane, the more it is affected by gravity. Thrust is the force that moves a plane forward. Experiment with a toy airplane or glider. When you throw the plane, you provide the thrust. In a real airplane, the thrust comes from the propellers or the jet engine.

The forward movement produced by the thrust causes air to move across the surface of the wing, and this creates lift, an upward force that keeps the plane in the air. This is how an airplane can fly.

As the airplane moves forward, the air creates drag on the plane and slows it down. A disadvantage of drag is that it is a force that tries to prevent motion. A plane needs more thrust than drag if it is to fly.

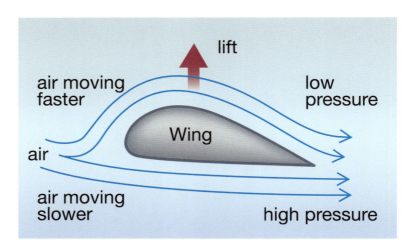

Drag can be used by the pilot to control the plane. An airplane has flaps on the wings and the tail, and the pilot turns these to increase the drag on one side of the plane or the other in order to steer it. When it comes in to land at an airport, the flaps are used to
5 deliberately slow the airplane down.

Words & Phrases

4. **steer**
[stiər]

   direction
[dirékʃən]

Post-Reading Activity

On the drawing of the airplane, draw arrows that show the direction in which each of the forces—gravity, thrust, lift, and drag—is acting. Describe the effect of each force on an airplane.

UNIT 1

Pre-Reading Activity  Part 3

Do you think a jet engine could be used to propel an object across the land or over water? Describe how this would work. Search the Internet to find out whether jet engines have been used to power cars or boats.

Words & Phrases

2. **propel**
   [prəpél]
5. **sticky**
   [stíki]
6. **straw**
   [strɔː]
8. **feed**
   [fiːd]

Make your own simple jet engine to show how it produces a force that propels an object through the air. You will need the following materials:

1. A piece of thread long enough to stretch across your room.
2. Two pieces of sticky tape.
3. A drinking straw.
4. A balloon.

Feed one end of your thread through the drinking straw. Attach one end of the thread to one side of the room, and the other end to the other side of the room at the same height from the ground. Make sure that the thread is stretched tight. Slide the straw to one end of the thread, and stick the two pieces of tape across the straw so that they stick out on both sides of it. Now blow up the balloon and hold onto the neck of it tightly so that no air escapes. Position the balloon under the straw with the neck pointing at the wall, and attach the balloon to the straw with the tape. Now let go off the balloon. What happens?

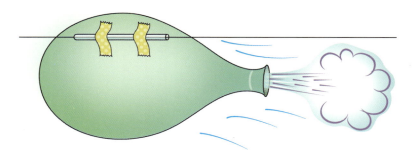

Post-Reading Activity

After your investigation, write a report summarizing your results.

UNIT 1

Comprehension

A Write "T" if the statement is true and write "F" if the statement is false.

1. Flying a model plane cannot help show you how moving air lifts up a wing.
2. Gravity comes from the propellers or the jet engine.
3. Drag can be used by a pilot to control a plane.
4. Airplanes have large jet engines that produce a powerful stream of air.

1. (   )   2. (   )   3. (   )   4. (   )

B Listen to the sentences and fill in each blank.

1. Tape cotton _____ to two lightweight balls and hang them about 15 cm apart.

2. Try _____ air through the space between the balls. _____ what happens.

3. As the airplane moves _____, the air creates drag on the plane and slows it down.

4. A _____ of drag is that it is a force that tries to prevent motion.

5. Make your own simple jet engine to show how it _____ a force that propels an object through the air. You will need the following _____.

Grammar & Vocabulary

A Fill in each blank so that the sentence will match the content of the text.

1. Gravity is the force that acts _____ all objects and pulls them toward the center of the Earth.

2. A plane needs more thrust _____ drag if it is to fly.

3. Attach the paper clip _____ the tail of the plane.

B Complete each sentence using the correct form of the verb in parentheses.

1. Moving air around their wings _____ carry them high into the sky. (help)

2. Try _____ air through the space between the balls. (blow)

3. The forward movement _____ by the thrust causes air to move across the surface of the wing. (produce)

スマートフォンでQRコードを読み取ってみよう

次のUnit 2はQRコードを開発した日本人技術者の題材です。本課の音声が目次(p.3)のQRコードに入っているのでダウンロードしてみましょう。

「Google play(playストア)」・「App Store」でQRコードのリーダーをインストールしてください。QRコードのリーダーを起動し,「QRコードを読み取る」と自動的にURLにジャンプします。ID:**kosen** パスワード:**scitech29**を入力すると,ウェブページが表示されます。リンクをタップすると,ストリーミング再生されます。※ダウンロードには通信費が必要です。

スマートフォンをお持ちでない方やうまくダウンロードできない方は,パソコンから下記のURLにアクセスしてください。

http://www.kairyudo.co.jp/contents/03_ko/eigo/ko-sen/data/data.htm

UNIT 2 The History of QR Code

Do you know that QR Code was invented by engineers from a Japanese company? In this unit, we are going to learn about how QR Codes work and the background of their development.

Pre-Reading Activity

Part 1

Read the QR Code on page 3 with your mobile phone and download the audio data for Unit 2.

Words & Phrases

2. **commodity** [kəmάdəti]
3. **foodstuff** [fúːdstʌf]
4. **cash register** [kǽʃ rèdʒistər]
4. **checkout** [tʃékàut]
5. **require** [rikwáiər]
5. **manually** [mǽnjuəli]
6. **cashier** [kæʃíər]
8. **lighten** [láitn]
8. **burden** [bə́ːrdn]

In the 1960s, when Japan entered its high economic growth period, supermarkets selling a wide range of commodities from foodstuffs to clothing began to spring up in many neighborhoods. Cash registers that were then used at checkout counters in these stores required the price to be keyed in manually. Because of this, many cashiers suffered from numbness in the wrist and carpal tunnel syndrome. "Cashiers desperately longed for some way to lighten their burden." The invention of barcodes provided a solution to this problem.

As the use of barcodes spread, however, their limitations became apparent as well. The most noticeable was the fact that a

The History of QR Code

barcode can only hold 20 alphanumeric characters or so of information. Out of a strong desire to develop a code that could be read easily as well as being capable of holding a great deal of information, Mr. Masahiro Hara, in charge of the development of QR Code, set out to develop a new 2D code. He dared to try this with only one other person as his team member.

The greatest challenge for the team was how to make reading their code as fast as possible. One day, he hit on the idea that their problem might be solved by adding positional information indicating the existence of a code to be read. This was how the position detecting pattern made up of square marks came into being. A year and a half after the development project was initiated and after innumerable and repeated trials and error, QR Code capable of coding about 7,000 numerals with the additional capability to code *kanji* characters was finally created. This code could not only hold a great deal of information, but it could also be read more than 10 times faster than other codes. In 1994, DENSO WAVE announced the release of QR Code. QR in the name stands for quick response, expressing the development concept for the code, whose focus was placed on high-speed reading.

p.12
Words & Phrases
10. **limitation**
[lìmətéiʃən]

Notes
6. **numbness**
[nʌ́mnis]
無感覚

6. **carpal tunnel syndrome**
[káːrpəl tʌ́nl sìndroum]
手根管症候群

p.13
Words & Phrases
3. **be capable of ~**
4. **in charge of ~**
5. **2D**
= two dimensions
5. **dare**
[deər]
9. **positional**
[pəzíʃənl]
11. **detect**
[ditékt]
12. **initiate**
[iníʃièit]
13. **innumerable**
[injúːmərəbl]
13. **trial and error**
14. **numeral**
[njúːmərəl]
14. **additional**
[ədíʃənl]
15. **capability**
[kèipəbíləti]

Notes
1. **alphanumeric**
[ælfənjuːmérik]
英数字の
17. **DENSO WAVE**
デンソーウェーブ(日本の企業)

● バーコード

● QRコード

Post-Reading Activity

Make pairs and talk about where you can see QR Codes in your daily life.

UNIT 2

Pre-Reading Activity

Make pairs and discuss what functions you want to add to QR Code.

Words & Phrases

1. **effort** [éfərt]
1. **adopt** [ədápt]
2. **contribute** [kəntríbjuːt]
4. **transaction** [trænsǽkʃən]
5. **societal** [səsáiətl]
5. **trend** [trend]
6. **demand** [dimǽnd]
7. **transparent** [trænspéərənt]
7. **traceable** [tréisəbl]
8. **pharmaceutical** [fὰːrməsúːtikəl]
9. **merchandise** [mɔ́ːrtʃəndàiz]
9. **indispensable** [ìndispénsəbl]
10. **medium** [míːdiəm]
14. **stipulate** [stípjulèit]
14. **standardize** [stǽndərdàiz]
15. **approve** [əprúːv]

Notes

2. **Kanban**
   かんばん方式での部品納入の作業指示書

    As a result of Mr. Hara's efforts, QR Code was adopted by the auto industry for use in their electronic *Kanban*, and it contributed greatly to making their management work efficient for a wide range of tasks: from production, to shipping, to the issuing of transaction slips. Moreover, in response to a newly-emerging societal trend where people demanded that the industries' production processes be made transparent—partly to make products traceable—food, pharmaceutical and contact lens companies began to use the code to control their merchandise. QR Code became an indispensable medium that could store a great deal of information about these processes.

    Since QR Code is an open code that anyone can use, it is used not only in Japan, but also in countries all over the world. As rules for its use were stipulated and the code was standardized, its use spread further. In 1999, it was approved as a standard 2D code by

商品に取り付けられたタグのQRコードを読み取ると情報が表示される。

The History of QR Code

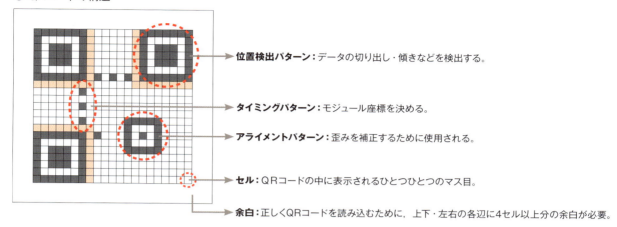

the Japan Industrial Standards Committee and made a standard 2D symbol on the Japan Automobile Manufacturers Association's EDI standard transaction forms. Furthermore, in 2000, it was approved by the ISO as one of its international standards. At present, the use of QR Code is so widespread that it is no exaggeration to say that it is used everywhere in the world.

　　In 2012, eighteen years after its creation, QR Code won a prize in the Media for Industry category of the Good Design Award. This was the first time that the designers of QR Code were acknowledged and honored publicly for their innovative methods spreading how and where QR Code can be used. In reply to a question asking him what kind of people he hopes will use QR Code, Mr. Hara said: "I don't dare specify what kind of people will use it. I just want to let a lot of people use QR Code, come up with new ways of using it with them, and put these ideas into practice. This is my policy."

Words & Phrases

2. **automobile** [ɔ́ːtəməbíːl]
5. **widespread** [wáidspréd]
5. **exaggeration** [igzædʒəréiʃən]
8. **category** [kǽtəgɔ̀ːri]
10. **acknowledge** [æknɑ́lidʒ]
10. **publicly** [pʌ́blikli]
11. **in reply to ~**
13. **specify** [spésəfài]
15. **put ~ into practice**

Notes

2. **EDI**
   = Electronic Data Interchange
   商取引のための各種情報
4. **ISO**
   = International Organization for Standardization
   国際標準化機構
8. **Good Design Award** [əwɔ́ːrd]
   グッドデザイン賞

Post-Reading Activity

Make your own business card with a QR Code which has information about you.

UNIT 2

Comprehension

A Write "T" if the statement is true and write "F" if the statement is false.

1. In the 1960s, Mr. Hara invented barcodes that could hold 20 alphanumeric characters.
2. Some companies began to use QR Code to control their products.
3. QR Code was approved by the ISO as an international standard in 1997.
4. In 2012, QR Code won the Good Design Award and its designers were publicly acknowledged.
5. Mr. Hara said that he wanted a lot of people to use QR Code to improve it.

1. (　)　2. (　)　3. (　)　4. (　)　5. (　)

B Listen to the passage and fill in each blank.

　　The engineers of DENSO WAVE started to develop a code that could be read easily and hold a great deal of ¹i_____. One and a half years later, they finally created QR Code that could code about ²*_____ numerals. As a result of their efforts, it was ³a_____ by the auto industry. Mr. Hara, the leader of QR code development, said that he wanted a lot of people to use it for the sake of its ⁴i_____.

*write a number that you can hear

The History of QR Code

Grammar & Vocabulary

A Fill in the blank with the appropriate choice.

1. The new computer is (   ) understanding human language.
   (a) able of
   (b) able to
   (c) capable of
   (d) capable to

2. He is in (   ) of information technology at a securities company.
   (a) charge
   (b) order
   (c) response
   (d) spite

3. JIS (   ) for Japanese Industrial Standards.
   (a) expresses
   (b) shows
   (c) indicates
   (d) stands

4. She demanded that he (   ) the whole truth.
   (a) told her
   (b) tell her
   (c) told to her
   (d) tell to her

5. Please let me (   ) if there is anything that I can do to help.
   (a) know
   (b) to know
   (c) knowing
   (d) known

B Put the words in the parentheses in the right order.

1. (the accident / is / happened / how / this).

2. She (only / also French / not / but / English / speaks).

3. It (that / can skate / so / is / we / cold) here.

4. He (with / came / our problem / to / a solution / up).

5. (by / can / anyone / used / this umbrella / be).

Basic Terms for Science — Mathematics 1

1 Match figures and words. Choose the proper words below.

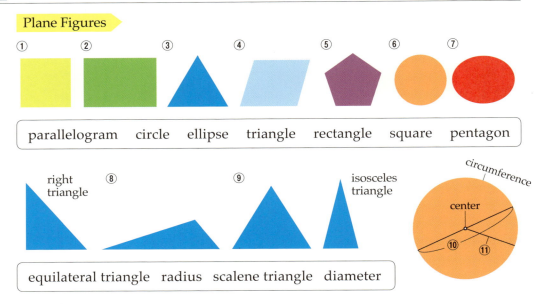

parallelogram   circle   ellipse   triangle   rectangle   square   pentagon

equilateral triangle   radius   scalene triangle   diameter

2 Match figures and words. Choose the proper words below.

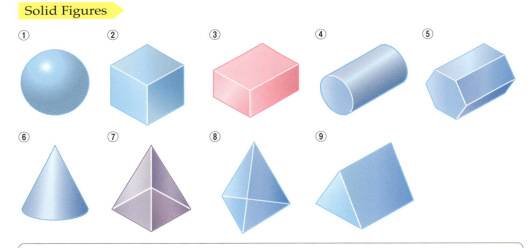

square-based pyramid   column (cylinder)   hexagonal prism
triangular-pyramid   cube   cone   rectangular   triangular-prism   sphere

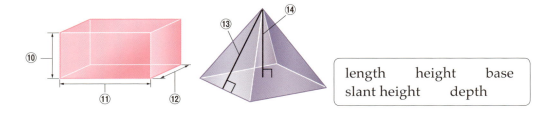

length   height   base
slant height   depth

Basic Terms for Science Mathematics 2

1 Choose the proper words below.

Angles and Lines

( ) angle   ( ) angle   ( ) angle

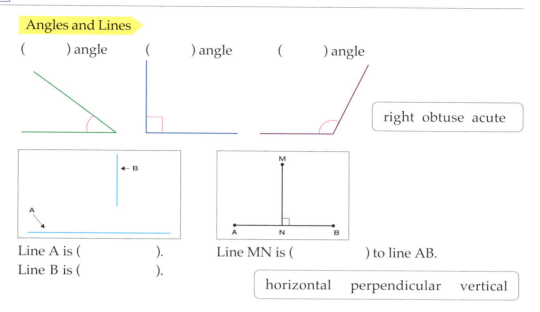

right obtuse acute

Line A is (   ).
Line B is (   ).

Line MN is (   ) to line AB.

horizontal   perpendicular   vertical

2 Choose the proper words below.

( ) chart   ( ) chart

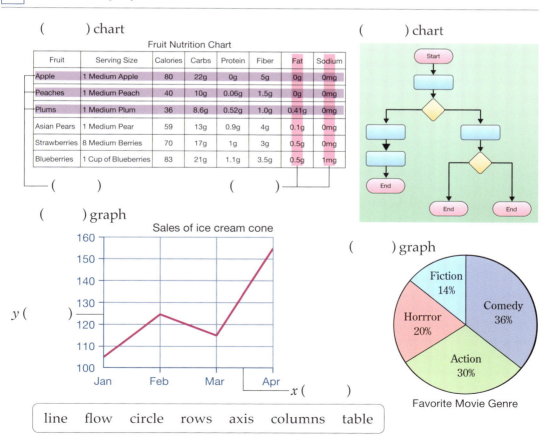

( ) graph

y ( )

x ( )

( ) graph

Favorite Movie Genre

line   flow   circle   rows   axis   columns   table

UNIT 3 Codes and Ciphers

It is very important not only for spies but for all of us to keep and send some kind of information secretly. In this chapter, we are going to look at some classical codes and ciphers.

Pre-Reading Activity

What kind of information do we need to or want to hide from others?

Words & Phrases

- **cipher**
  [sáifər]
2. **substitution**
  [sÀbstətjúːʃən]
6. **emerge**
  [imə́ːrdʒ]
7. **scramble**
  [skrǽmbl]
8. **conceal**
  [kənsíːl]

Notes

9. **Morse code**
  [mɔ́ːrs kóud]
  モールス信号

  The words "code" and "cipher" are sometimes used as if they mean the same thing. But they do not. A code is a substitution, such as "The Big Cheese lands at Happy tomorrow." We do not know who the "Big Cheese" is, or where "Happy" is. But if you notice the president of France landed at Heathrow Airport the day after such a message, a pattern might begin to emerge. On the other hand, ciphers are scrambled messages. In a cipher, a plain-text message is concealed by replacing the letters according to a pattern. Even Morse code is, in fact, a cipher. Following are some examples of simple ciphers, which are very useful and fun when you send secret messages to someone.

Codes and Ciphers

1. The Caesar Shift Cipher

Here is a simple alphabet code to start with. This is called "The Caesar Shift Cipher" used by Julius Caesar, a Roman general and statesman. Each letter is moved along by a number—say four. A becomes E, J becomes N, Z becomes D, and so on. The number is the key to the cipher here. Caesar could agree on the number with his generals in private and then send encrypted messages knowing they could not be read without the key. For example, "The dog is sick" becomes "WKH GRJ LV VLFN," with the number three as the key. (see *figure 1*) As a first cipher it works well, but someone who really wanted to break the code could simply plod their way through all twenty-five combinations.

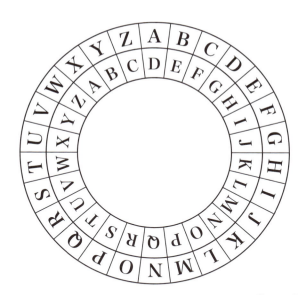

figure 1

2. Numbers

The second one is called "Numbers." For example, A = 1, B = 2, C = 3, etc., all the way to Z = 26. Messages can be written using those numbers. This cipher is probably too simple to use on its own; however, if you combine it with a Caesar code number, it can

UNIT 3

Words & Phrases
1. tricky
   [tríki]
5. overheat
   [òuvərhíːt]
7. beforehand
   [bifɔ́ːrhænd]

Notes

decrypt
[diːkrípt]
解読する

suddenly become very tricky. In the basic method, "The dog is better" would be "20 8 5—4 15 7—9 19—2 5 20 20 5 18," which looks difficult but isn't. Add a Caesar cipher of 3, however, and the message becomes "3 23 11 8—7 18 10—12 22—5 8 23 23 8 21," which should overheat the brain of your younger brothers or sisters trying to break the encryption. To make this even harder to break, the key could be agreed beforehand in private.

Plain-text Alphabet	A	B	C	D	E	F	G	H	I	J	K	L	M	N	O	P	Q	R	S	T	U	V	W	X	Y	Z
Numbers	1	2	3	4	5	6	7	8	9	10	11	12	13	14	15	16	17	18	19	20	21	22	23	24	25	26
Caesar Cipher of 5	6	7	8	9	10	11	12	13	14	15	16	17	18	19	20	21	22	23	24	25	26	1	2	3	4	5

table 1

Post-Reading Activity

(1) Using the Caesar Shift Cipher, encrypt and decrypt the flowing tables with key 3.

encrypt

c	o	f	f	e	e

decrypt

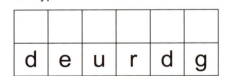

(2) Decrypt the following message, made by Numbers with Caesar Shift Cipher of 5.

14 25—2 14 17 17—23 6 14 19

Codes and Ciphers

Pre-Reading Activity  Part 2

Have you ever read or watched any fiction (novels, movies, etc.) on secret messages? Or do you know any historical events in which codes and ciphers played important roles?

3. Alphabetic ciphers

There are many types of these. Most of them depend on the way the alphabet is written out, which is agreed beforehand. Using the sequence in *table 2*, for example, "How are you?" would become
5 "UBJ NER LBH?"

A	B	C	D	E	F	G	H	I	J	K	L	M
N	O	P	Q	R	S	T	U	V	W	X	Y	Z

table 2

According to the sequence in *table 3*, "How are you?" would become "SLD ZIV BLF?" It's worth remembering that even simple ciphers are not obvious at first glance.

A	B	C	D	E	F	G	H	I	J	K	L	M	N	O	P	Q	R	S	T	U	V	W	X	Y	Z
Z	Y	X	W	V	U	T	S	R	Q	P	O	N	M	L	K	J	I	H	G	F	E	D	C	B	A

table 3

Most famous of the alphabet variations is "a code stick"—
10 another one used by the Romans. Begin with a strip of paper and wind it around a stick, such as a pencil. It is important that the sender and the receiver both have the same type.

Words & Phrases
1. **alphabetic**
   [ǽlfəbétik]
4. **sequence**
   [síːkwəns]
7. **worth ~ing**
8. **obvious**
   [ábviəs]
8. **glance**
   [glǽns]
10. **strip**
    [strip]
11. **wind**
    [wáind]
12. **sender**
    [séndər]

UNIT 3

Words & Phrases

3. **unwound**
[ʌ̀nwáund]

4. **gibberish**
[dʒíbəriʃ]

11. **stud**
[stʌd]

11. **rotate**
[róuteit]

13. **approximately**
[əpráksəmətli]

14. **accurately**
[ǽkjurətli]

17. **random**
[rǽndəm]

Notes

9. **diameter**
[daiǽmətər]
直径

13. **segment**
[ségmənt]
区切り

figure 2

Here the word "HEATHROW" is written down the length of the pencil, with a couple of letters per turn of the strip (see *figure 2*). When the tape is unwound, the same pen is used to fill in the spaces between the letters. It should now look like gibberish. The idea is that when it is wound back on to a similar stick, the message will be clear.

Another famous cipher variation is called "cipher wheels." Using a pair of compasses, cut four circles out of a card, two large and two small—5 inch (12 cm) and 4 inch (10 cm) diameters work well. For both pairs, put one on top of the other and punch a hole through with a butterfly stud. They should rotate easily. A circle = 360 degrees. There are twenty-six letters in the alphabet, so the spacing for the segments should be approximately 14 degrees. Mark off the segments as accurately as you can for all four circles. When they are ready, write the normal alphabet around the outside of the large circles in the usual way—A to Z. For the inner circles, mark the letters in random order. As long as the matching code wheel is done in the same way, it doesn't matter where the letters go. The code sequence will begin with the two-letter combination that shows the positions of the wheels—AM or AF, for example. You should end up with a cipher-wheel encrypter that can only be read by someone with the other wheel. For example, if you use the cipher wheel in *figure 3*, "AQ R QV IQBBE" is decoded as "I am happy."

Notes

2. **decode**
   [diːkóud]
   解読する

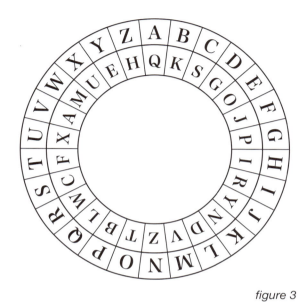

figure 3

Post-Reading Activity

(1) Make a code-stick cipher and send a simple message to your friend.

(2) Crack the following, which was encrypted with the cipher wheel in *figure 3*.

"AQ FIO KTU RC IRGGOZ XZGOW FIO FWOO"

_____

_____

UNIT 3

Comprehension

A Write "T" if the statement is true and write "F" if the statement is false.

1. The art of breaking ciphers is called "codes" in the modern world.
2. According to the article, it is not so difficult to solve the Caesar Shift Cipher.
3. To decipher Numbers, we need to number letters of the alphabet in order.
4. When using "a code stick," the sender sends a stick wrapped with a strip of paper to the receiver.
5. When making "cipher wheels," we need four circles which are the same size.

1. (   )   2. (   )   3. (   )   4. (   )   5. (   )

B Fill in the blanks and listen and check your answers.

1. A plain-text was _____ by _____ the letters according to a _____.
2. To make this even _____ to break, the key could be _____ beforehand _____ private.
3. Begin with a _____ of paper and _____ it around a _____.
4. Here the word "Heathrow" is written down the _____ of the pencil, with a _____ of letters _____ turn of the strip.
5. For both pairs, _____ one on top of the other and _____ a hole through with a butterfly _____.

C Listen to the passage and fill in each blank.

There are many types of ¹c_____ and ciphers. One of the oldest types of ciphers is the Caesar Shift Cipher, which was ²n_____ after famous Julius Caesar. Caesar used it to send ³s_____ messages to his generals. In this cipher, each letter is replaced by a letter ⁴f_____ along in the ⁵a_____.

Grammar & Vocabulary

A Choose the word below to match each definition.

1. To join or mix two or more things together
2. A long, thin piece of wood
3. Words that have no meaning or are impossible to understand
4. To wrap something around something else
5. A part or section of something
6. A particular way of doing something
7. A straight line through the center of a circle, from one side to another
8. To come out from an enclosed or dark space, or from a position where you could not be seen
9. To turn around and around like a wheel
10. A following of one thing after another in a regular or fixed order

(a) method   (b) emerge   (c) combine   (d) sequence   (e) stick
(f) wind   (g) gibberish (h) diameter (i) rotate   (j) segment

1. (   ) 2. (   ) 3. (   ) 4. (   ) 5. (   )
6. (   ) 7. (   ) 8. (   ) 9. (   ) 10. (   )

B Put the words in the parentheses in the right order.

1. An original message is concealed (according / by / letters / replacing / the) to a pattern.

   ....

2. The hidden message could (be / not / read / the / without) key for it.

   ....

3. It doesn't (come / from / matter / you / where).

   ....

UNIT 4 Can Robots Be Good Companions?

Hiro is a college student in the USA. One day, he visited a laboratory managed by Dr. Kevin, who is a roboticist at Hiro's college. There, they talked about humans and their relationship with robots.

Pre-Reading Activity

What is the first thing that comes to your mind when you think of a robot?
Explain to your friend what a robot is. When, where, and how do they work?

Words & Phrases
- laboratory [lǽbərətɔ̀ːri]
- roboticist [roubɑ́təsist]
- come to *one's* mind
7. context [kɑ́ntekst]
9. humanoid [hjúːmənɔ̀id]
10. resemblance [rizémbləns]
10. furthermore [fə́ːrðərmɔ̀ːr]

Notes
7. artificial intelligence [àːrtəfíʃəl intélədʒəns] 人工知能

(*H: Hiro; Dr. K: Dr. Kevin*)

H: Hello, Dr. Kevin. I'm interested in studying robotics. Could you please tell me, what can we learn from robots?

Dr. K: As you know, robots have become an important part of our everyday activities. Some people think of robots as machines that can help us in our daily lives, while others think of them in the context of artificial intelligence. Indeed, there are as many different types of robots as there are tasks for them to perform. Some advanced robots are called humanoid robots because of their resemblance to human beings. Furthermore, there are robots that can express and perceive emotions. What do you

Can Robots Be Good Companions?

think? Could humanoid robots become just like humans in the future?

H: Well, probably not. I can think of two reasons why. First, we humans can use language. However, language among humanoid robots is limited to what is programmed into them by engineers, and even this language is often quite repetitive. Second, we have emotions. It is said that there are six basic emotions common to all human cultures: fear, disgust, anger, surprise, happiness, and sadness. Moreover, the non-verbal communication of emotions is not a cultural phenomenon but a universal one. Certain robots exhibit some emotional behavior; however, a robot does not "feel" in any real sense.

Dr. K: I see. That is a very good line of reasoning. Using language is what distinguishes human beings from the rest of creation. Did you know that from birth, babies can feel interest, distress, disgust, and happiness, and can communicate these through facial expressions and physical postures? Attuning themselves to the aural expression of emotions is the very first step for humans learning social interaction.

Words & Phrases

6. **repetitive** [ripétətiv]
8. **disgust** [disgʌ́st]
9. **non-verbal** [nὰnvə́ːrbəl]
10. **phenomenon** [finάmənὰn]
11. **exhibit** [igzíbit]
13. **reasoning** [ríːzəniŋ]
14. **distinguish** [distíŋgwiʃ]
15. **distress** [distrés]
17. **posture** [pʌ́stʃər]
17. **attune** [ətjúːn]
18. **aural** [ɔ́ːrəl]
19. **interaction** [ìntərǽkʃən]

音声を認識し，笑った表情を見せるヒト型ロボット「HRP-4C」。人間らしい動作や対話ができる。（2009年茨城県つくば市の産業技術総合研究所）

Post-Reading Activity

Form a group, and discuss the advantages and disadvantages of using robots in our lives.

UNIT 4

Pre-Reading Activity — Part 2

If you were living alone except for a robot companion, what daily life topics would you talk about with the robot?

Words & Phrases

2. **infant** [ínfənt]
3. **affection** [əfékʃən]
4. **on the contrary**
5. **simulate** [símjulèit]
9. **associate** [əsóuʃièit]
10. **isolation** [àisəléiʃən]
10. **loneliness** [lóunlinəs]
13. **astronaut** [æstrənɔ̀ːt]
16. **extensive** [iksténsiv]
17. **interactive** [ìntəræktiv]
17. **capability** [kèipəbíləti]
19. **dialogue** [dáiəlɔ̀ːg]
21. **cue** [kjuː]
25. **utter** [Átər]

Notes

2. **pronounced** [prənáunst] 顕著な
12. **Kirobo** キロボ(ロボットの名)
14. **Koichi Wakata** 若田光一(1963-) 日本の宇宙飛行士
14. **Pepper** ペッパー(ロボットの名)

Dr. K: An interesting study found that three- to seven-month-old infants showed a more pronounced response to sad sounds than to neutral ones. Humans often use affection to communicate with one another, and emotions affect human action. On the contrary, robots simulate emotions by acting.

H: Interesting.

Dr. K: Have you ever heard about "social robots"? They can use language to communicate with humans within the social and cultural contexts associated with their role. Social robots can help people avoid isolation and loneliness. We are now in the era of social robots.

H: Yes, I have heard of them. I know "Kirobo," the world's first talking astronaut robot, which was sent into space to serve as a companion to astronaut Koichi Wakata, and "Pepper," which was designed to read and respond to users' moods.

Dr. K: According to an extensive survey of social robots, a socially interactive robot requires specific capabilities: it has to be able to express and perceive emotions, communicate through high-level dialogue, and be able to recognize other robots. Furthermore, it needs to be capable of establishing and maintaining social relationships using natural cues such as gazes, gestures, and so on.

H: These aspects are precisely how we humans act when we communicate with others. My question is: How does a robot decide which sentence is more appropriate to utter at a certain

Can Robots Be Good Companions?

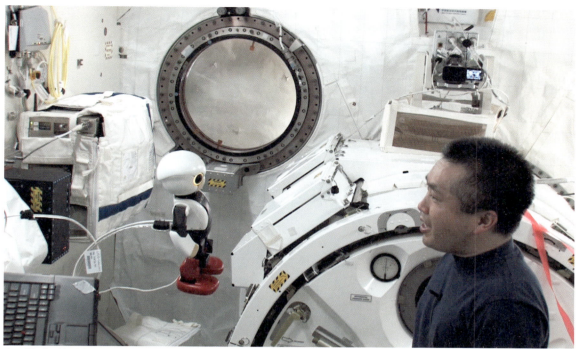

キロボと会話実験を行う国際宇宙ステーション(ISS)内に滞在する若田光一さん。実験では若田さんが「キロボ君に会うのをずっと楽しみにしてたよ」と語りかけると，キロボも「僕もずっと会いたかった」と返答。「無重力に慣れたかな」と尋ねられると，「もう慣れたよ。全然平気」と答えた。（2013年）

moment?

Dr. K: Let's consider a hypothetical situation. If you see a close friend sitting in your classroom looking depressed, who proceeds to tell you that he/she did badly at an important job interview, what would you say to your close friend?

H: Hmm.... Let me think about this.

Words & Phrases

2. **hypothetical**
[hàipəθétikəl]

3. **depressed**
[diprést]

recognition
[rèkəgníʃən]

device
[diváis]

Post-Reading Activity

Using voice recognition on your phone or personal computer, tell your phone or PC that you are not happy right now. What kind of conversation did you have with your device?

UNIT 4

Pre-Reading Activity

Your friend seems to be upset. If you create a robot whose task is to comfort people, what conversation would you imagine and program into the robot? Draw an example situation in the four-frame comic below. If you need to, you can choose one expression from the box below and use it in the dialogue.

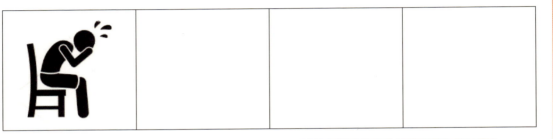

I understand how you must feel. / Don't push yourself too hard. / I've been there. / Better luck next time! / I am here to help. / Other (your choice)

Words & Phrases

upset
[ʌ̀psét]

3. **encouragement**
[inkə́ːridʒmənt]

6. **incident**
[ínsədənt]

9. **self-esteem**
[sélfistíːm]

9. **sympathy**
[símpəθi]

11. **crucial**
[krúːʃəl]

12. **interpersonal**
[ìntərpə́ːrsənl]

Notes

6. **severity**
[səvérəti]
深刻さ

15. **i.e.**
[áiíː]
すなわち

H: I would say, "You did the best you could. I know you're a hard worker. Forget about it, and move on to the next challenge!"

Dr. K: That is positive encouragement. Some people may feel encouraged by your words, while others may not. Responses can also differ depending on whether the friend is male or female. The severity of the incident and the psychological distance between you and your friends also affect how they perceive your words. However, in order to respect your friend's self-esteem in private situations, you could show sympathy, offer some encouragement, and even help.

H: I learned that the way we respond to situations is crucial for good interpersonal relationships among people. It is difficult for humans to do this well, let alone robots. What need is there for humans to constantly develop robots with this particular set of abilities, i.e., with regard to emotion recognition and response?

Dr. K: I guess we will see in the years to come. We do consider emotions and language when communicating with one another in social contexts. Humans also adjust their tone of voice, body language, and behavior in social interactions. The human mind is an extremely complex organ. My answer to your first question—What can we learn from robots?—is that if robots achieve human-level intelligence and become useful companions to us, this might be a key to better understanding human nature.

Words & Phrases
4. **behavior**
 [bihéivjər]
5. **organ**
 [ɔ́ːrgən]

Post-Reading Activity

Having done pre-reading activities 2 and 3, you have an idea of a social robot. Please share your ideas about how a robot of this kind could comfort people in class.

UNIT 4

Comprehension

A Write "T" if the statement is true and write "F" if the statement is false.

1. There are as many robots as there are applications for them.
2. Babies cannot attune themselves to the aural expressions of emotions.
3. Social robots are designed to establish social relationships and help people avoid isolation.
4. People's perception of what a person says is not affected by psychological distance.
5. The development of social robotics can contribute to understanding human behavior.

1. (   )   2. (   )   3. (   )   4. (   )   5. (   )

B Fill in the blanks and listen and check your answers.

Although some animals can exhibit ¹e_____ through facial expression or other behavior, humans can perceive and express ¹e_____ by using language. There are as many types of robots nowadays as there are tasks for them to ²p_____. Surprisingly, there are robots that can use language to communicate with humans within the ³s_____ and cultural contexts associated with their role. They are called ³s_____ robots. They can ⁴r_____ one another, and possess histories based on their own experiences. Humans naturally use affection to communicate with one another. However, socially ⁵i_____ robots learn emotions by communicating with humans. Responding ⁶a_____ to others' emotions is sometimes difficult, even for humans. Studying robots and challenging the limits of their capabilities may be crucial to better understanding human nature.

Grammar & Vocabulary

A Choose the appropriate word from the two choices in parentheses.

1. I'm starting a new job next week. I'm very (exciting / excited) about it.
2. I've been working very hard all day and now I'm (exhausting / exhausted).
3. Joe is very good at telling funny stories. He is very (amusing / amused).
4. Julia has learned Japanese very quickly. She has made (astonishing / astonished) progress.
5. The big earthquake was a really (terrifying / terrified) experience.

1. (   )   2. (   )   3. (   )   4. (   )   5. (   )

B Choose the appropriate word from the box below.

How do you describe a person who:

1. feels happy about something. The person is _____ .
2. is very sad and without hope. The person is _____ .
3. has a strong feeling of dislike or disapproval for something. The person is _____ with something.
4. is very angry. The person is _____ .
5. feels unhappy, anxious, or annoyed. The person is _____ .

> upset / furious / pleased / disgusted /
> calm / comfortable / depressed

Science Lab

1 Magnus Effect
マグヌス効果

? Shoot a ball through a right curved pipe. Which direction does this ball go?
A. left   B. straight   C. right

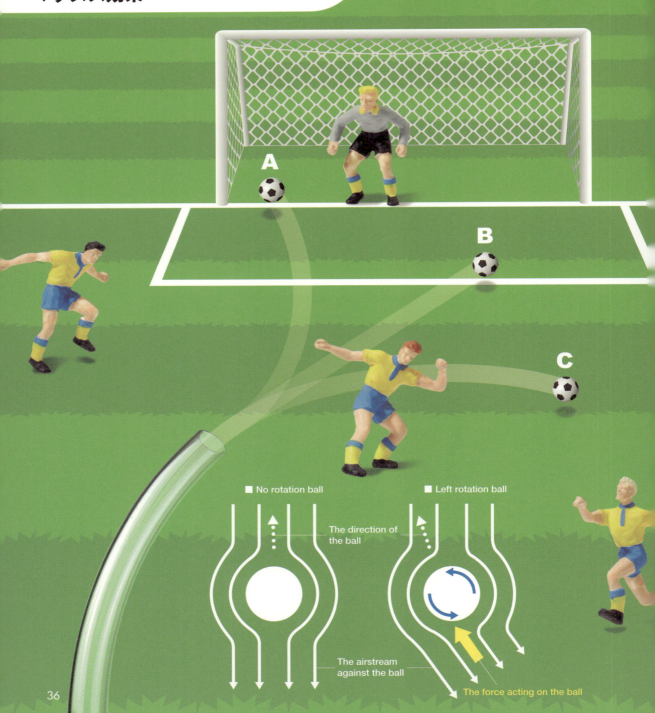

■ No rotation ball   ■ Left rotation ball

The direction of the ball

The airstream against the ball

The force acting on the ball

Science Lab

Preparation

① a vinyl tube (Inner Diameter: 15 mm, Length: about 20 cm)
② 2 to 3 foam balls (Diameter: 12 mm)

Procedure

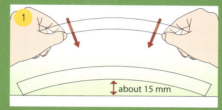

Bend a vinyl tube into a curve. If you can't do it well, bend it in warm water.

※Be sure not to inhale the ball.

Put a foam ball in the inlet of the tube, and blow sharply. Try blowing in different directions, and watch the track of the ball.

Trivia

The secret of breaking balls lies in the Magnus effect. Breaking balls show their effect in baseball or soccer. The change of the direction of the ball is due to its rotation, that is the Magnus effect. You give right spin to a ball when you want to turn the ball right, and left spin to turn the ball left. The faster the ball rotates, the more it breaks.

---

curve カーブさせる
pipe 管,パイプ
direction 方向
preparation 準備物
vinyl ビニール
diameter 直径
procedure 手順
bend 曲げる
inlet 入口
sharply すばやく
track 軌道
trivia 豆知識
due to ～ ～のため
spin 回す
rotate 回転する
breaking ball 変化球

2 Supercooling

過冷却

Preparation

① 8 aluminum foil cups for chocolate (Base Diameter: 2.4 cm, Depth: 1.5 cm)
② plastic container (about the size of a lunch box, with a lid if possible)
③ about 100g of ice (ice cube in a freezer)
④ a heavy plastic bag
⑤ about 20g of salt (a tablespoon and over)
⑥ a pair of tweezers, a hammer, a scale, a tablespoon, water (tap water)

Science Lab

 **Procedure**

Put ice in a plastic bag and break it into pieces with a hammer.

Put the broken ice in a plastic container. Sprinkle salt over the ice and mix them.

Make an airspace between the plastic container and the bottom with the lid of the container or the like in order to prevent the heat conduction from the bottom.

Prepare four pairs of two-ply aluminum foil cups. Put 2 to 3 ml (half a teaspoon) water in each cup. You don't have to use purified water. You can use tap water.

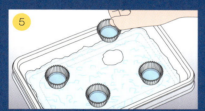

Make four holes in the ice prepared in step ② and put the cups on them horizontally.

※Note that the cups contact ice equally around them.

Observe for 5 to 10 minutes. When water in one of the cups freezes, put a small piece of ice into each of the other cups, and water suddenly changes into ice.

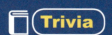 **Trivia**

A cloud is made up of very small water drops (cloud drops). A cloud becomes rain after cloud drops freeze and become bigger with other cloud drops around. But water hardly freezes and remains supercool high in the sky where the temperature is 0 ℃ and under. Then there is an idea that we make rain by artificially making the cloud drops freeze. Artificial rain is under study in countries where there is a problem of water shortage.

aluminum
アルミニウム

foil
ホイル

container
容器

lid
ふた

freezer
冷凍庫

tablespoon
大さじ

tweezer
ピンセット

sprinkle
振りかける

prevent
防ぐ

heat conduction
熱伝導

two-ply
2枚重ねの

teaspoon
小さじ

purify
精製する

purified water
精製水

horizontally
水平に

remain
(〜の)ままである

artificially
人工的に

artificial
人工的な

Lab Report
実験レポート

　今まで行った実験のレポートを書こう。
　実験レポートは、なぜその実験を行ったのか、その実験によってどのようなことがわかったのかということを明らかにする必要があります。Scientific Method という方法を使って、レポートを完成させよう。
　Scientific Method を使うと以下のような流れでレポートを書くことができます。

実際にSupercooling（過冷却）の実験レポートを書いてみよう。

❓ Question

　We cooled down the water in a PET bottle for a day in a refrigerator and then for two hours in a freezer. When we took it out and gave it a mild shock, it suddenly froze. Why did this happen?

📋 Background Research

　When the water is cooled down slowly, it sometimes does not freeze at 0 °C, and sometimes not even at −10 °C and below. This is called supercooling. When supercool water is given a "trigger" to freeze, it changes into ice.

⚙ Construct Hypothesis

　もし水をゆっくりと冷やしていき、軽い衝撃を与えれば、水は瞬時に凍る。

　When the water is cooled down slowly and given mild shock, it froze in a moment.

🧪 Test with Experiments
◆ **Preparation**
　① 8 aluminum foil cups for chocolate (Base diameter: 2.4 cm, Depth: 1.5 cm)
　② plastic container (about the size of a lunch box, with a lid if possible)

③ about 100g of ice (ice cube in a fridge)
④ a heavy plastic bag
⑤ about 20g of salt (a tablespoon and over)
⑥ a pair of tweezers, a hammer, a scale, a tablespoon, water (tap water)

◆ **Procedure**

1. Put ice in a plastic bag and break it into pieces with a hammer.
2. Put broken ice in a plastic container. Sprinkle salt over ice and mix them.
3. Make space of air between the plastic container and the bottom with the lid of the container or the like in order to prevent the heat conduction from the bottom.
4. Prepare four pairs of two-ply aluminum foil cups. Put 2 to 3 ml (half a teaspoon) water in each cup. You don't have to use purified water. You can use tap water.
5. Make four dents on ice prepared in step 2 and put the cups on them horizontally.
   * Note that the cups contact ice equally around them.
6. Monitor for 5 to 10 minutes. When water in one of the cups freezes, put small piece of ice into the rest of the cups, and water suddenly changes into ice.

Results

複数のアルミカップを同時に冷やし，その中の1つが凍ったのを見計らってほかのカップに氷を落としたところ，水が氷にかわっていった。

We cooled down all the aluminum foil cups at the same time, and at the timing when one of them froze, we put ice into the rest and the water changed into ice.

Analyze Results / Draw Conclusion

4つのうち1つのアルミカップの中の水は自然と凍ったということは，ほかの水は過冷却になっていたと考えられるため，推論は正しかったといえる。

The fact that the water in one of the four cups froze without shock means the water in the rest was supercool. Therefore we can say that our reasoning was right.

Exercise

マグヌス効果についても実験レポートを書いてみよう。

Basic Terms for Science — Mathematics 3

1 Match signs and words.

- + · · square root
- − · · equal (not equal)
- × · · number
- ÷ · · plus (addition)
- = (≠) · · factorial
- # · · pi
- ( ) · · minus (subtraction)
- π · · division
- √ · · greater (less) than
- ≦ (≧) · · parentheses
- > (<) · · greater (less) than or equal to
- ! · · multiplication

How do you read it?

common fractions
- $\frac{1}{4}$ a quarter
- $\frac{1}{3}$ a third
- $\frac{2}{5}$ two fifths

decimal fractions
- 0.25 zero point two five
- 0.4   zero point four

algebra
- a^2 a squared (a to the second power)
- a^3 a cubed (a to the third power)
- a^n a to the n-th power
- $\sqrt{a}$ the square root of a
- $\sqrt[n]{a}$ the n-th root of a

2 Choose the proper words.

① ( )
  $a \times b = c$ a ( ) by b equals c.

② ( )
  $a \div b = c$ a ( ) by b equals c.

③ ( )
  $a + b = c$ a ( ) b equals c.

④ ( )
  $a - b = c$ a ( ) b equals c.

⑤ $x^2 + y^2 = z^2$ x ( ) plus y ( ) equals z ( )
  ※Pythagorean theorem

⑥ $x^3 + y^3 = z^3$ x ( ) plus y ( ) equals z ( )
  ※Fermat's last theorem

⑦ $x(y+z)$ x ( ) the ( ) of y plus z
  [x open ( ) y plus z close parenthesis]

⑧ $y = -3x^2 + 4x$ y ( ) minus [( )] three x squared plus four x

- a. multiplied
- b. divided
- c. cubed
- d. times
- e. equals
- f. addition
- g. subtraction
- h. division
- i. minus
- j. sum
- k. negative
- l. parenthesis
- m. multiplication
- n. plus
- o. squared

Basic Terms for Science — Chemistry

1 Write Japanese words corresponding to the English words below.

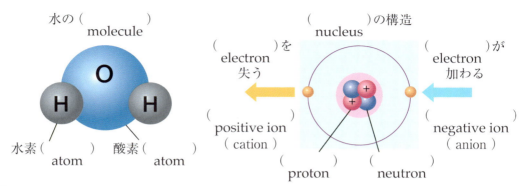

水の（　　）molecule
水素（　　）atom　　酸素（　　）atom
（　　）の構造 nucleus
（　　）を electron 失う
（　　）が electron 加わる
（　　）positive ion (cation)
（　　）negative ion (anion)
（　　）proton　（　　）neutron

2 Choose the names of the atoms and the compounds below.

Na（ナトリウム）（　）　　K（カリウム）（　）　　Sn（スズ）（　）
Hg（水銀）（　）　　S（硫黄）（　）　　CO_2（二酸化炭素）（　）
NaCl（塩化ナトリウム）（　）　　　　CuO（酸化銅）（　）
CO（一酸化炭素）（　）　　H_2O_2（過酸化水素）（　）　　P_2O_5（五酸化リン）（　）

1. sodium　2. carbon dioxide　3. tin　4. copper oxide　5. mercury
6. sodium chloride　7. phosphorus pentoxide
8. sulfur　9. carbon monoxide　10. hydrogen peroxide　11. potassium

3 Choose the descriptions corresponding to the reactions below.

$2HgO \rightarrow 2Hg + O_2$　（　）
$2FeO + C \rightarrow 2Fe + CO_2$　（　）
$2H_2 + O_2 \rightarrow 2H_2O$　（　）

ⓐ Hydrogen plus oxygen makes water.
ⓑ Mercury oxide decomposes to mercury and oxygen.
ⓒ Iron oxide plus carbon makes iron and carbon dioxide.

4 Write the Japanese names of the instruments below.

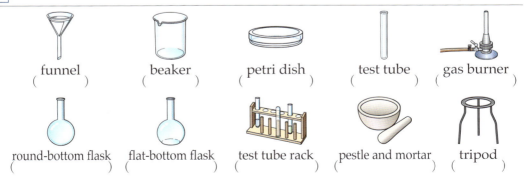

funnel（　　）　beaker（　　）　petri dish（　　）　test tube（　　）　gas burner（　　）
round-bottom flask（　　）　flat-bottom flask（　　）　test tube rack（　　）　pestle and mortar（　　）　tripod（　　）

43

UNIT 5 Laterality: Left-handed versus Right-handed

Are you left-handed, or right-handed? This chapter will let you discover that your body is less than total in its devotion to its favored side. But how far does this bias in your body extend? Discuss with your fellow students how left-sided or right-sided you are and think about products that solve problems related to laterality.

Pre-Reading Activity

Part 1

Most of human behavior is asymmetrical, however, is there a good reason why right-handedness is preferred?

Words & Phrases

devotion
[divóuʃən]

bias
[báiəs]

asymmetrical
[èisəmétrikəl]

3. clap
[klæp]

4. cock
[kɑk]

10. bilateral
[bailǽtərəl]

Notes

laterality
[lætərǽləti]
左右差

　　A great deal of human behavior is asymmetrical. Laterality is demonstrated whenever an action demands more from one side of the body than the other. Every time we wave, wink, clap, shake a fist, cock an eyebrow, put an eye to a telescope, fold our arms, or cross our legs, we are forced to favor one side more than the other. 5

　　The problem starts early in infancy and goes through a strangely complex series of stages. At 12 weeks, babies usually use both hands with equal vigor, but by 16 weeks they mostly favor the left hand when making contact. By 24 weeks they have changed again and show a strong shift back to the bilateral use of both hands. 10

Then at 28 weeks, they become unilateral once more, shifting this time to the right hand. Stability begins, at last, at around the age of 4 years, and grows in strength until, finally, at the age of 8 years, the child is fixed in its permanent condition, with one hand strongly dominant over the other.

The most peculiar feature of this long sequence is that the end result is a population of human beings showing a strong bias towards right-handedness. Roughly 9 out of every 10 school-children are naturally right-handed and 1 out of 10 is naturally left-handed. No one has ever satisfactorily explained why this curious ratio should be typical of our species. It remains one of the minor mysteries of human life.

Inevitably, the majority have repeatedly attempted to suppress the unfortunate minority (even though, today, there must be somewhere in the region of 200 million left-handers). Many cultures in the past—and some, even today—have encouraged their school-teachers and their parents to force their left-handed children into righteous ways. Enlightened education authorities in many countries have now abandoned this policy and permit children to follow their natural tendencies; but, even so, the left-handers are still looked upon as not quite "right."

Post-Reading Activity

In a group, discuss the merits of being left-handed or right-handed in our daily lives.

UNIT 5

Pre-Reading Activity

Finally, most of human beings show a strong bias towards right-handedness. How did the term "right-handed" originate in the first place?

Words & Phrases

- originate [ərídʒənèit]
2. gross [grous]
2. oversimplification [òuvərsìmpləfikéiʃən]
2. equate [ikwéit]
4. synonymous [sinánəməs]
5. despite [dispáit]
10. simplify [símpləfài]
12. itching [ítʃiŋ]
13. scratch [skrætʃ]
14. interlock [ìntərlák]
14. uppermost [ápərmòust]
15. applaud [əplɔ́ːd]
17. imaginary [imǽdʒənèri]
24. forefinger [fɔ́ːrfìŋgər]

Notes

1. inherent [inhíərənt]
   内在して, つきもので

Inherent in all general discussions of left and right handedness is one gross oversimplification. This is the equating of leftness and rightness with the act of writing. The very term "right-handed" has become synonymous with holding a pen or pencil in the right hand, despite the fact that there are many other one-sided actions being performed throughout any ordinary day.

It is worth carrying out a simple test on yourself to see just how left-sided or right-sided you are. How far does this bias in your body extend? Are you left-eyed, or right-eyed? Left-eared or right-eared? Here is a simplified 10-point test you can apply to yourself:

(1) Imagine the center of your back is itching. Which hand do you use to scratch it?

(2) Interlock your fingers. Which thumb is uppermost?

(3) Imagine you are applauding and start clapping your hands. Which hand is uppermost?

(4) Wink at an imaginary friend straight in front of you. Which eye does the winking?

(5) Put your hands behind your back, one holding the other. Which hand does the holding?

(6) Someone in front of you is shouting, but you cannot hear the words. Cup your ear to hear better. Which ear do you cup?

(7) Count to three on your fingers, using the forefinger of your other hand. Which forefinger do you use?

Laterality

(8) Tilt your head over on to one shoulder. Which shoulder does it touch?

(9) Fold your arms. Which forearm is uppermost?

(10) Fixate a small, distant object with your eyes and point directly at it with your forefinger. Now close one eye. Now change eyes. Which eye was open when the fingertip remained in line with the small object? (When the other eye, the non-dominant one, is open and the dominant eye is closed, the finger will appear to move to one side of the object.)

If you have always spoken of yourself as right-handed or left-handed, you will probably now have discovered that your body is less than total in its devotion to its favored side. If you are right-handed, the chances are that you were not able to answer "right" ten times. If you are a parent or a school-teacher, then this is something worth bearing in mind whenever you feel tempted to criticize a left-handed child.

Words & Phrases
1. **tilt** [tilt]
3. **forearm** [fɔ́ːràːrm]
4. **fixate** [fíkseit]
6. **fingertip** [fíŋɡərtìp]
16. **bear** [beər]
16. **tempt** [tempt]
17. **criticize** [krítəsàiz]

(10)利き目の見分け方

Post-Reading Activity

In a group, discuss the result of the 10-point test.

UNIT 5

Pre-Reading Activity

We have learned a few things about laterality so far. Now let's think about products that solve problems related to it. What would you make? Share your ideas with your friends.

Words & Phrases

2. **inventor**
   [invéntər]
6. **withdraw**
   [wiðdrɔ́:]
7. **compared to**
9. **prototype**
   [próutətàip]
10. **improve**
    [imprú:v]
11. **determined**
    [ditə́ːrmind]
12. **mass-produce**
    [mǽsprədjúːs]
13. **manufacturer**
    [mæ̀njufǽktʃərər]
16. **accompany with**
16. **assert**
    [əsə́ːrt]
23. **displace**
    [displéis]
24. **vertically**
    [və́ːrtikəli]
25. **clutch**
    [klʌtʃ]

Notes

16. **ergonomic grip**
    [ə̀ːrgənámik gríp]
    人間工学に基づいたグリップ
21. **hook**
    [huk]
    手首をかぎや留め金のように曲げて書く方法
22. **underwriter**
    [ʌ́ndərràitər]
    紙を左に30度から45度程度回転させて書く方法
23. **overwriter**
    [óuvərràitər]
    紙を右に30度から45度程度回転させて書く方法
24. **fist**
    [fist]
    ペンを手の平で握るようにして書く方法

Left-handed pen makes life easier

Tony Hemmings, a British inventor, helped design a pen for left-handed people. His 13-year-old daughter had difficulty learning to write, which led him to create a left-handed pen when she started school. He was worried that his left-handed daughter was ⁵ withdrawing into her shell when she had trouble in writing compared to other children. He created the "Swan Neck Pen" prototype for her, and her progress improved. By the time she was 13, ¹⁰ her father had become determined to mass-produce the design, and it is now produced by a UK manufacturer.

Swan Neck Pen

Left-handers have a difficult time writing

The attractive point of the pen is its design: an "S" curve ¹⁵ accompanied with an ergonomic grip. The design team asserts that such a shape enables people who are left-handed to grab it and be able to easily write something at once.

For a long time, left-handed writers have had difficulty seeing what they are writing. In an effort to see what they are writing, the ²⁰ styles they have adopted are as follows: "the hook," where left-handers can hook their hand at the wrist; "the underwriter" positions the page at different angles; "the overwriter" displaces the page to the left sometimes vertically; "the fist" where people clutch the pen tightly in a fist. ²⁵

the hook the underwriter the overwriter the fist

Laterality

Words & Phrases

1. **comment** [kάment]
6. **standardize** [stǽndərdàiz]
6. **primary** [práimeri]
10. **eliminate** [ilímənèit]
11. **discomfort** [diskÁmfərt]
11. **ashamed of**
12. **additional** [ədíʃənl]
17. **universal** [jùːnəvə́ːrsəl]

Tony Hemmings commented that it was hard to imagine how many left-handers had trouble writing. He hoped that the pen would be helpful for more than one billion left-handed people throughout the world as well as people in the UK.

5　His neighbor, Mike Deacon, who designed the pen, said that his dream was to standardize the "Swan Neck Pen" in all primary schools so it can be easily used by both left- and right-handed writers. This would be the beginning of an age when all left-handed children came to use a pen as easily as right-handed children.

10　Mike hoped that using this pen would finally eliminate any discomfort from feeling ashamed of being a left-handed writer.

One additional factor that makes the inventor and the design team excited is that the pen can be used not only by left-handers, but also by right-handers who write from right to left. When they
15　write in this way, the "Swan Neck Pen" helps them to see what they are writing.

Therefore, we can say that it is a universal design pen for both left-handers and right-handers because all you need to do is to hold the pen. For left-handers, in particular, the pens can solve a
20　lot of inconvenient styles, such as "the hook," "the underwriter," "the overwriter" and "the fist."

Post-Reading Activity

Explain the merits of the "Swan Neck Pen."

UNIT 5

Comprehension

A Write "T" if the statement is true and write "F" if the statement is false.

1. All creatures have laterality problems and the ratio of leftness and rightness is similar to those of human beings.
2. About 9 out of 10 school-children are naturally left-handed, but they gradually become right-handed.
3. The term "right-handed" is derived from the act of writing.
4. According to the writer, children should be forced to write with the right hand, regardless of their natural tendency.
5. Tony Hemmings thinks that the "Swan Neck Pen" would be useful for not only left-handers but also right-handers.
6. It was Tony Hemmings who designed the pen.

1. (   )   2. (   )   3. (   )   4. (   )   5. (   )   6. (   )

B Fill in the blanks and listen and check your answers.

A great ¹d_____ of human behavior is asymmetrical. ²L_____ is demonstrated as most humans ³p_____ one side of their body over the ⁴o_____ when they do something in their daily lives.

It's one of the ⁵m_____ mysteries of human life that the ⁶r_____ of right-handed pupils to left-handed pupils is 9:1.

So why did the ⁷t_____ "right-handed" originate in the first place? It has become ⁸s_____ with the act of writing, ⁹d_____ many other one-sided actions being performed by people throughout any ¹⁰o_____ day.

There are many products, however, that are being created to ¹¹p_____ an end to any ¹²s_____ of left-handers.

50

Grammar & Vocabulary

A Choose the word below to match each definition.

1. having the same, or nearly the same, meaning
2. not equal for example in the way each side or part behaves
3. more important, powerful than other things
4. to give up completely

> (a) dominant (b) asymmetrical (c) synonymous (d) abandon

1. (   )   2. (   )   3. (   )   4. (   )

B Put the words in the parentheses in the right order.

1. Mike wins (we / game / every / the / time / play).

2. Computers in education (to / more / enable / people / us / reach) in the world.

3. Lisa (the / as / is / on / looked / leader) on the subject.

4. Despite (went / rain, / for / the / out / we) a walk.

5. I think (visiting / worth / the / twice / is / temple).

C Choose the appropriate word from the two choices in parentheses.

1. Please go (with / through) the following stages.
2. We encourage him (to / with) read newspapers.
3. I had difficulty (to control / controlling) my anger.
4. Ted solved the questions with (ease / easily).
5. We must put (an end / ends) to all these problems.

UNIT 6 The *Challenger* Disaster: Why Did It Happen?

The *Challenger* Disaster is an important topic as a case study of "Engineering Ethics." In this case, engineers requested that managers postpone the lift-off of the space shuttle *Challenger* for security reasons. Managers, however, didn't listen to their request and decided to go ahead with the lift-off for cost and scheduling reasons. Read carefully about how managers and engineers came to make such a decision.

Pre-Reading Activity

Part 1

1. Look at the picture above. What happened to *Challenger*?
2. Why do you think the *Challenger* Disaster happened?
3. What do you think is important for engineers to avoid this kind of disaster?

Words & Phrases
- **disaster** [dizǽstər]
- **ethic** [éθik]
- **postpone** [poustpóun]
2. **unveil** [ʌ̀nvéil]
2. **reusable** [rìːjúːzəbl]
2. **manned** [mænd]

In 1976, the National Aeronautics and Space Administration (NASA) unveiled the world's first reusable manned spacecraft, known as the space shuttle. Five years later, shuttle flights began when *Columbia* traveled into space on a 54-hour mission.

Challenger, NASA's second space shuttle to enter service, 5 embarked on its maiden voyage on April 4, 1983, and made a total of nine voyages prior to 1986. That year, it was scheduled to launch on January 22, carrying a seven-member crew.

The *Challenger* Disaster

The mission's launch from Kennedy Space Center at Cape Canaveral, Florida, was delayed for six days due to weather and technical problems. The morning of January 28 was unusually cold, and engineers warned their superiors that certain components—particularly the rubber O-rings that sealed the joints of the shuttle's solid rocket boosters—were vulnerable to failure at low temperatures. However, these warnings were ignored by management members, and at 11:39 a.m. *Challenger* lifted off.

Seventy-three seconds later, hundreds on the ground, including the families of the astronauts on board, stared in disbelief as the shuttle exploded in a bi-pronged plume of smoke and fire. Millions more watched the heart-wrenching tragedy unfold on live television. Within instants, the spacecraft broke apart and plunged into the ocean, killing its entire crew, traumatizing the nation and throwing NASA's shuttle program into turmoil.

Shortly after the disaster, President Ronald Reagan appointed a special commission to determine what went wrong with

固体燃料補助ロケット
(solid rocket booster)
外部燃料タンク (external tank) の両側に1本ずつ取り付けられ，スペースシャトル打上げ時のほとんどの推力を担う。打上げから約2分後に分離され，パラシュートで降下し海へ着水した後，回収される。

Oリング (O-ring)
※スペースシャトルで使用されているものとは異なる

p.52
Words & Phrases
2. **spacecraft** [spéiskræft]
6. **embark** [imbá:rk]
7. **prior to ~**
7. **launch** [lɔ:ntʃ]

Notes
6. **maiden voyage** [méidn vɔ́iidʒ] 処女航海

p.53
Words & Phrases
2. **due to ~**
4. **superior** [səpíəriər]
5. **component** [kəmpóunənt]
5. **joint** [dʒɔint]
6. **vulnerable** [vʌ́lnərəbl]
7. **ignore** [ignɔ́:r]
10. **including** [inklú:diŋ]
10. **disbelief** [dìsbilí:f]
11. **explode** [iksplóud]
11. **plume** [plu:m]
12. **tragedy** [trǽdʒədi]
12. **unfold** [ʌnfóuld]
13. **plunge** [plʌndʒ]
14. **traumatize** [trɔ́:mətàiz]
15. **turmoil** [tɔ́:rmɔil]
16. **appoint** [əpɔ́int]
17. **commission** [kəmíʃən]
17. **determine** [ditɔ́:rmin]

UNIT 6

p.53
Notes

5. **O-ring**
 [óuriŋ]
 密封に使われる断面が○形の
 機械部品

6. **solid rocket booster**
 固体燃料補助ロケット

11. **bi-pronged**
 [baipró:ŋd]
 2本に分かれた

12. **heart-wrenching**
 [há:rtrèntʃiŋ]
 悲痛な

16. **Ronald Reagan**
 [ránld réigən]
 (1911-2004)
 米国第40代大統領

p.54
Words & Phrases

1. **corrective**
 [kəréktiv]

7. **potential**
 [pəténʃəl]

7. **be aware of ～**

8. **take action**

Notes

5. **Morton Thiokol**
 [mɔ́:rtn θáiəkɔ̀:l]
 米国の企業

Challenger and to develop future corrective measures. Headed by former secretary of state William Rogers, the commission included former astronaut Neil Armstrong and former test pilot Chuck Yeager.

The commission found that Morton Thiokol, the company 5 that designed the solid rocket boosters, had ignored warnings about potential issues. NASA managers were aware of these design problems but also failed to take action.

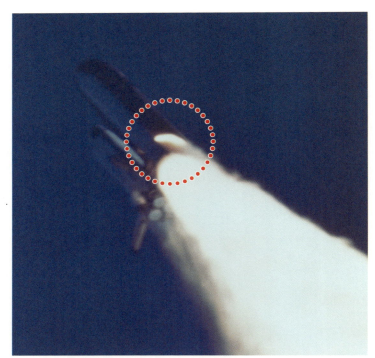

打ち上げから約59秒後のチャレンジャー。右側の固体燃料補助ロケットからガスが漏洩し，引火している。（赤丸部分）

Post-Reading Activity

Make a post-disaster summary of the *Challenger* tragedy, and discuss in a group the reasons why managers from the company and NASA ignored warnings from engineers about the O-rings.

The *Challenger* Disaster

Pre-Reading Activity   Part ❷

1. Have you ever experienced a feeling such as "I can do this even if it looks impossible," when you keep succeeding or winning? Give an example.
2. Do you know the concept of "Informed Consent"? Give an example where this is important.

A great many researchers investigated the hidden human factors that caused the misjudgment responsible for the *Challenger* disaster. Two researchers in India identified three facts that should be considered regarding this misjudgment.

Fact 1: NASA experienced plenty of success before the *Challenger* disaster.

From the mid-1970s, the Space Shuttle project became NASA's primary focus and progressed quickly. In the span of just 57 months between April 1981 and January 1986, 24 shuttle missions involving four different shuttles—*Columbia*, *Challenger*, *Discovery* and *Atlantis*—were successfully completed one after another at an incredible average of about one mission every ten weeks. This success story drove and was driven by NASA's legendary "can-do" attitude.

The organization even readily accepted challenges that might drain resources from other aspects of the space program, and sometimes disrupt routine operations.

Fact 2: Managers and engineers were aware of the problems with O-rings since 1977, but never considered them a threat.

A major problem related to the O-rings was discovered by Thiokol engineers in 1985, one year before the lift-off: the effect of low temperatures on O-ring resilience. Resilience here refers to the

Words & Phrases
1. **investigate** [invéstəgèit]
2. **misjudgment** [mìsdʒʌ́dʒmənt]
3. **identify** [aidéntəfài]
5. **plenty of ~**
8. **primary** [práiməri]
8. **progress** [prəgrés]
8. **span** [spæn]
12. **incredible** [inkrédəbl]
13. **legendary** [lédʒəndèri]
14. **attitude** [ǽtitjùːd]
16. **drain** [drein]
16. **resource** [ríːsɔːrs]
16. **aspect** [ǽspekt]
17. **disrupt** [disrʌ́pt]
17. **routine** [ruːtíːn]
20. **threat** [θret]
21. **related to ~**
23. **resilience** [rizíljəns]

Words & Phrases

1. **regain**
 [rigéin]
2. **squeeze**
 [skwi:z]
4. **continuously**
 [kəntínjuəsli]
5. **involve**
 [inválv]
7. **immediate**
 [imí:diət]
8. **dedicate**
 [dédikèit]
9. **exception**
 [iksépʃən]
9. **observation**
 [ùbzərvéiʃən]
12. **redesign**
 [rì:dizáin]

Notes

6. **vice president**
 [váis prézədənt]
 副社長

ability of an O-ring to regain its original shape after it has been squeezed and released. It was found that at 100°F (about 37°C), the O-ring functioned properly but as the temperature was lowered, it continuously lost resilience and ability to function.

Roger Boisjoly, a Thiokol engineer directly involved with the tests, wrote a letter to his Vice President of Engineering, Robert Lund, in July, 1985, saying that "we should take immediate action to dedicate a team to solve the problem."

With the exceptions of such individual observations, managers and engineers at both Thiokol and NASA in general continued to believe that though the O-ring problem was important and needed to be addressed, it was safe to fly without a redesign.

打ち上げ前，氷が貼りついた発射台の整備塔

Post-Reading Activity

Discuss in a group why one engineer's individual suggestion was not accepted by all responsible people at the company and NASA.

The *Challenger* Disaster

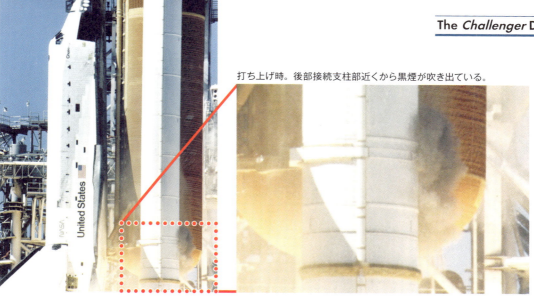

打ち上げ時。後部接続支柱部近くから黒煙が吹き出ている。

Pre-Reading Activity

Part 3

What is a paramount value for managers and that of engineers? Give an example.

Fact 3: NASA and Thiokol managers proceeded with the launch on January 28, 1986, despite strong appeals from Thiokol engineers to stop.

Engineers at Thiokol appealed to managers at Thiokol and NASA organization on the evening of January 27 not to launch on the 28—and to delay the launch—owing to low ambient temperature. The engineers were very concerned about potential O-ring malfunction since the ambient temperatures on the 27 were much lower than those experienced during earlier launches.

When engineers expressed their concerns in a meeting with managers, the manager Larry Mulloy was unhappy with this and stated that the engineers' data was inconclusive. He did not support their recommendations. The Thiokol managers then had a "private" five-minute meeting in the presence of the engineers during which they decided to make a "management decision." Engineers were excluded from the final decision.

Words & Phrases

paramount
[pǽrəmàunt]

1. **proceed**
[prəsíːd]

2. **despite**
[dispáit]

6. **ambient**
[ǽmbiənt]

8. **malfunction**
[mælfʌ́ŋkʃən]

12. **inconclusive**
[ìnkənklúːsiv]

13. **recommendation**
[rèkəmendéiʃən]

16. **exclude**
[iksklúːd]

UNIT 6

Words & Phrases

2. **responsibility**
[rispɑ̀nsəbíləti]

5. **capacity**
[kəpǽsəti]

6. **obligation**
[ɑ̀bləɡéiʃən]

7. **welfare**
[wélfɛər]

7. **canon**
[kǽnən]

8. **urge**
[əːrdʒ]

13. **priority**
[praiɔ́ːrəti]

14. **loyalty**
[lɔ́iəlti]

15. **override**
[òuvəráid]

16. **singlemindedness**
[síŋɡlmáindidnis]

17. **pursuit**
[pərsúːt]

17. **delightfully**
[diláitfəli]

18. **wholly**
[hóulli]

20. **irresponsibility**
[irispɑ̀nsəbíləti]

20. **magnificently**
[mæɡnífəsntli]

21. **dedication**
[dèdikéiʃən]

22. **unfortunate**
[ʌ̀nfɔ́ːrtʃənət]

22. **consequence**
[kɑ́nsəkwèns]

Notes

7. **ASME**
アメリカ機械学会

Engineers' Responsibility

To understand the responsibility of engineers more deeply, we should remember key elements of the professional responsibilities between engineers and society. As engineers test designs for ever-increasing speeds, loads, capacities and the like, they must always be aware of their obligation to society to protect the public welfare. The first canon in the ASME (American Society of Mechanical Engineers) Code of Ethics urges engineers to "hold paramount the safety, health and welfare of the public in the performance of their professional duties." Every major engineering code of ethics reminds engineers of the importance of their responsibility to keep the safety and well-being of the public at the top of their list of priorities.

Although company loyalty is important, it must not be allowed to override the engineer's obligation to the public. It is a sad fact that loyalty sometimes invites singlemindedness. Single-minded pursuit of a goal is sometimes delightfully romantic, even a real inspiration. But this is not wholly appropriate for engineers, whose impact on the safety of the public is so very significant. Irresponsibility, whether caused by selfishness or by magnificently unselfish loyalty and dedication, can nevertheless have most unfortunate consequences."

Post-Reading Activity

Discuss in a group what you could have done to delay the launch if you had been a member of this project.

The *Challenger* Disaster

Comprehension

A Write "T" if the statement is true and write "F" if the statement is false.

1. When the space shuttle *Challenger* lifted off, the weather was warm and clear.
2. A great many people from all over the world were watching the tragedy on TV.
3. One reason for the tragedy might be that there had been a lot of successes in the Space Shuttle project before the tragedy.
4. The Thiokol managers rejected suggestions from engineers because they did not rely on their personalities.
5. The most important duty of engineers is to keep paramount their loyalty to their company instead of the safety of society.

   1. (   )   2. (   )   3. (   )   4. (   )   5. (   )

B Fill in the blanks and listen and check your answers.

On January 28, 1986, the American shuttle orbiter *Challenger* broke up 73 seconds after [1] _____, bringing a devastating end to the spacecraft's 10th [2] _____. The disaster claimed the lives of all seven [3] _____ aboard. It was later determined that two rubber O-rings, which had been designed to separate the sections of the rocket booster, had failed [4] _____ to cold temperatures on the morning of the launch. The morning of January 28 was unusually cold, and engineers warned their managers that the rubber O-rings were [5] _____ to failure at low temperatures. However, these warnings were ignored, and at 11:39 a.m. *Challenger* lifted off. The tragedy and its aftermath received extensive media coverage and prompted NASA to temporarily [6] _____ all shuttle missions.

UNIT 6

Grammar & Vocabulary

A Choose the appropriate word or phrase from the box below.

1. The students are, with a few _____, all from Ibaraki Prefecture.

2. You should go to the dentist _____ once every three months.

3. His body failed _____ overwork.

4. I will attend the meeting _____ you.

5. She was good at physics _____ the fact that she found it boring.

> instead of / despite / owing to / exceptions / at least

B Put the words in the parentheses in the right order so that the sentence will match the Japanese translation.

1. 彼に危険を警告するために叫んだが、手遅れだった。

   I shouted (him / danger / to / of / warn / the), but it was too late.

2. 保護されないとすると、そのシステムはさまざまな攻撃に対して脆弱である。

   If not secured, (the system / various / vulnerable / attacks / is / to).

3. ジャックは次から次へと問題を解いていった。

   (one / Jack / another / after / solved / problem).

4. 私はその会社の立ち上げに携わってきた。

   (involved / with / the company / I / the start-up / was / of).

5. ロサンゼルスの気温は予想していたよりもはるかに涼しかった。

   The temperature in Los Angeles was (than / had / much / I / expected / cooler).

Column

Decision Making —意思決定—

　近年，技術者倫理教育が多くの企業で行われており，リスクマネージメントやコンプライアンスについて，より真摯に取り組む企業が増えてきています。イリノイ工科大学のマイケル・デイビス教授が整理した，Michael Davis' seven-step guide は，倫理に関わる意思決定をする際に役立ちます。この「7段階法」のアプローチを使って，行動案をさまざまな角度から検討してみましょう。まずは，以下の Case Study を通して考えてみましょう。

Case Study

フォード社製の自動車「ピント」の事例は，技術者倫理の話でよく取り上げられる事件です。Michael Davis' seven-step guide を使って，考えてみましょう。

Step 1 State the problem	倫理的問題を明確にする。
	技術者は，自分の関係者，取引先だけではなく，その車を使用する人々，その車を売る販売店，事故に巻き込まれる一般人のリスクまでを考慮したか。
Step 2 Check facts	事実関係を確認する。
	1972年，高速道路上で停止していたフォード社製のピントに，後続車両が衝突し，炎上したことによって，運転手が死亡し，同乗者が重傷を負った。その家族は，ピントの欠陥を理由として，フォード社を訴え，陪審で1億ドルの賠償の判決を得た。事故は，ピントの燃料タンクが後輪の車軸の外側にあり，後方から衝突をされた場合には，タンクが容易に変形し，ガソリンが漏れ出し火災が発生したことが原因と考えられる。
Step 3 Identify relevant factors	関連事項を特定する。
	フォード社は，日本からの安価な小型車に対抗すべく，ピントの車両価格を抑え，設計開始から2年程度の短期間で商品化することにした。この事件のほかにも，追突されて炎上した事例が，多数報告されていた。
Step 4 Develop list of options	考えられる行動案をリストアップする。
	① フォード社は，当時の安全規格に準拠しており，法律や規格の違反はないことを関係者へ報告する。 ② 試作段階での衝突実験で，後方からの衝突により，ガソリンの漏洩が発生して火災を引き起こす可能性を知っていた。まず，火災がおこる確率を調べ，その危険性を関係者へ知らせ，すでに車を購入した顧客へも知らせるよう，対策を考える。 ③ 事故が発生して，被害者に補償をするよりも，改修費用の方が，会社の損失が大きい。しかし，人命を軽視する対応にならないよう，燃料タンクの改善の重要性について関係者と情報を共有し，設計をやり直す。

Step 5 Test options	Step 4 の行動案を倫理的妥当性の観点から検討する。
	① **harm test**（危害テスト）： その行動案がもたらす危害はどうか。 ② **publicity test**（世間体テスト）： 自分の行動案が新聞やテレビで報道されたらどうなるか。 ③ **defensibility test**（自己防衛可能性テスト）： 公的な機関で自分の行動案について弁明できるか。 ④ **reversibility test**（可逆性テスト）： 自分がその行動案によって悪影響を受ける立場であっても、まだその行動案を支持するか。 ⑤ **virtue test**（徳テスト）： その行動案を頻繁に行った場合、どうなるか。 ⑥ **colleague test**（同僚による評価テスト）： その行動案を同僚に提案した場合、同僚はどう考えるか。 ⑦ **professional test**（専門家による評価テスト）： その行動案を専門家たちはどう考えるか。 ⑧ **organization test**（会社など自分が所属する組織による評価テスト）： 自分の所属する組織の倫理担当部署や顧問弁護士はどう考えるか。
	フォード社側から考えると、安全規格に適応しているので、欠陥は無いと主張することはできる。ピントは、後方からの衝突がなければ普通に使うことができる。しかし、この「後方衝突による炎上の危険性」は、車を購入する一般人には周知されず、その危険性がわかるのはエンジニアだけであった。車の運転手は、その危険性の認識がないままピントを購入し、事故にあったことになる。
Step 6 Make a choice	Step 1～5 の検討結果から行動案を決定する。
	安全基準を満たす車両が安全であるとは限らない。車の購入者へ事故の危険性の認識を持たせ、それでも「想定外」の出来事で購入者を死傷させてしまう場合は、製造販売を停止し、さらなる購入者の安全を優先する。
Step 7 Review steps	Step 1～6 のステップを再度検討し、その行動案が本当に問題を解決するのか確認する。
	フォード社は、使用者に炎上の危険性を知らせず、会社の利益を優先させて、製造・販売を続けた。裁判での賠償の根拠は、フォード社は、組織ぐるみで使用者の生存権を侵害したと判断された。基本的人権を侵害する重大行為ということであった。製品を製造・販売するときは、人命を守ることを一番に考えなければならない。

参照：Davis, Michael. *Ethics and the University*, New York: Routledge, pp.166-167, 1999.

✏️ Exercise

Unit 6 を読んで,「技術者」としてあなたはどのような意思決定をするのか考えてみましょう。

Step 1 State the problem	
Step 2 Check facts	
Step 3 Identify relevant factors	
Step 4 Develop list of options	
Step 5 Test options	**harm test**: **publicity test**: **defensibility test**: **reversibility test**: **virtue test**: **colleague test**: **professional test**: **organization test**:
Step 6 Make a choice	
Step 7 Review steps	

Basic Terms for Science — Physics 1

1 See the illustrations and choose the proper words below.

Properties of Forces

If A and B are in the same line as well as being equal and opposite, then the object will be in ( ).

| equilibrium | point of action | direction of force | magnitude of force |

2 Complete the explanation of the illustrations by choosing the proper words below.

Motion of Objects and Energy

The ( ) of the coin resists the change of its initial state, which is stationary. As a result, the coin does not move with the cardboard and falls into the glass because of ( ).

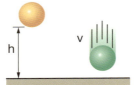

$$E_p = mgh$$

E_p = Potential Energy
m = Mass
g = Gravitational Field Strength
h = Vertical Height

$$E_k = \frac{1}{2} mv^2$$

E_k = Kinetic Energy
m = Mass
v = Speed

The orange ball has ( ) due to its height. The green ball has ( ) due to its velocity.

| gravity | inertia | action | reaction | potential energy |
| kinetic energy |

3 See the illustrations and choose the proper words below.

Light and Sound

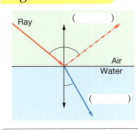
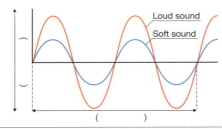

| reflection | refraction | cycles | amplitude |

Basic Terms for Science   Physics 2

1 Choose the proper words.

Circuit Diagrams

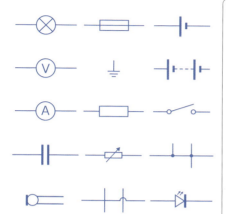

1. Filament lamp   2. Cell
3. Variable resistor   4. Ammeter
5. Microphone   6. Fuse
7. Capacitor
8. Junction of conductors (connected)
9. Voltmeter   10. Battery of cells
11. Earth
12. Crossing conductors (not connected)
13. Resistor   14. Switch
15. Light emitting diode (led)

2 Choose the correct option or answer.

Series and Parallel Circuits

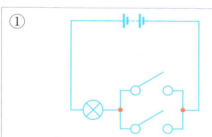

a. switches in series
b. switches in parallel
c. lamps in series

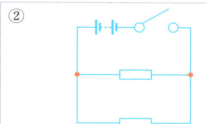

a. fuses in parallel
b. resistors in series
c. resistors in parallel

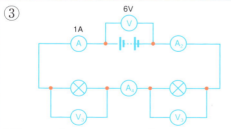

What is the correct reading on meter A2 in the circuit above?
a. 0.5A   b. 1A   c. 3A

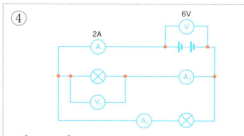

What is the correct reading on meter A3 in the circuit above?
a. 1A   b. 1.5A   c. 2A

③, ④ The lamps are identical.

UNIT 7 Lucky Number 113

Element 113, discovered by a RIKEN group led by Kosuke Morita, has become the first element on the periodic table found in Asia. Rewarding nearly a decade of painstaking work by Morita's group, a joint working party of international organizations has recommended that the group be given recognition for the discovery of the new element.

Pre-Reading Activity

In 1908, a Japanese scientist claimed to have discovered a new element, but his claim was later found to be wrong. Give what name and number the element is.

Words & Phrases
- periodic table
- painstaking [péinztèikiŋ]
2. massive [mǽsiv]
3. superheavy [sùːpərhévi]
4. proton [próutɑn]
4. nucleus [njúːkliəs]

  The heaviest element that occurs naturally on earth is uranium. More massive atoms have, however, been created in the laboratory. These so-called superheavy elements have more than 103 protons in their nucleus, but the complicated nuclear interactions between these subatomic particles makes such nuclei highly unstable. Further, these particles live for only a fraction of a second. A team of scientists across Japan and China led by RIKEN researcher Kosuke Morita has now seen an indirect signature of element 113 by measuring the particles generated when superheavy elements disintegrate. This new addition to the periodic table will improve our understanding of the building blocks of the universe.

An element is a group of substances, each having an identical number of protons in the nucleus. In the periodic table, elements are arranged in the order of the number of protons in each element. Element 1 is hydrogen, element 2 helium.

In the late 1980s, the group began using RIKEN's Linear Accelerator Facility and the GARIS ion separator, developed by Morita and his group, to explore new synthetic superheavy elements. The work of discovering new superheavy elements is very difficult, and the elements tend to decay extremely quickly —the isotopes of 113 produced at RIKEN lasted for less than a thousandth of a second. Researchers persevere, however, as the research is important for understanding the structure of atomic nuclei. Scientists hope that the work will lead eventually to the discovery of a so-called "island of stability" where elements with longer half-lives will be found.

The search at RIKEN for element 113 started in September 2003, when Morita's group began bombarding a thin layer of

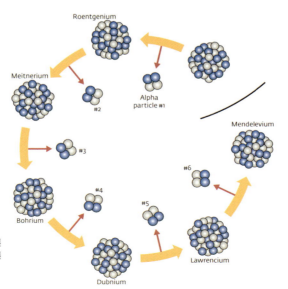

113番元素が6回のアルファ崩壊を経てメンデレビウムとなる崩壊経路の確認に成功した。
Ⓒ2012 RIKEN

UNIT 7

Words & Phrases

9. **fission**
 [fíʃən]
12. **conclusive**
 [kənklúːsiv]
14. **nuclide**
 [njúːklaid]
17. **characterize**
 [kǽriktəràiz]
18. **collide**
 [kəláid]
 colleague
 [kúliːg]

Notes

1. **bismuth**
 [bízməθ]
 ビスマス、蒼鉛
1. **zinc**
 [ziŋk]
 亜鉛
7. **alpha decay**
 [ǽlfə dikèi]
 アルファ崩壊。アルファ粒子（ヘリウム4の原子核で原子番号2,質量数4）を放出してより安定な核に崩壊すること。
8. **dubnium**
 [dúːbniəm]
 ドブニウム
16. **bohrium**
 [bóːriəm]
 ボーリウム
16. **lawrencium**
 [lɔːrénsiəm]
 ローレンシウム
18. **sodium**
 [sóudiəm]
 ナトリウム
19. **curium**
 [kjúəriəm]
 キュリウム

bismuth (element 83) with zinc (element 30) ions travelling at about 10% the speed of light. Theoretically, they would occasionally fuse, forming an atom of element 113. The team achieved its first success on July 23, 2004, less than a year after starting the experiment. Two atomic nuclei fused, leading to the creation of a nucleus of element 113, which quickly underwent four alpha decays, losing two protons each time to transform into dubnium-262 (element 105), which then underwent spontaneous fission. Less than a year later, on April 2, 2005, the team saw a second event—an identical decay to dubnium-262 (element 105) followed by fission. Though these were good demonstrations, they were not considered conclusive evidence for the existence of element 113, because the decay chain did not demonstrate "firm connections to known nuclides." The team pushed on with its efforts. In order to create a better picture of the decay chain from bohrium-266 (element 107) to lawrencium-258 (element 103), which had not been well characterized, the group performed a new experiment, where a sodium (element 11) beam was collided with a curium (element 96) target, creating borhium-266 (element 107) and its daughter nucleus, dubnium-262 (element 105). With this demonstration, the grounds for a stronger claim were laid. They just needed to wait to see an atom decaying through the alpha chain rather than spontaneous fission.

Post-Reading Activity

It took a long time to achieve the success in discovering new elements by the research group. Make pairs and discuss how you would continue the long-term work with your colleagues.

Pre-Reading Activity — Part ❷

Give some concrete examples of elements that are named after the nation where they were discovered.

Following the two initial events, however, the team's luck seemed to run dry. "For over seven years," says Morita, "we continued to search for data conclusively identifying element 113, but we just never saw another event. I was not prepared to give up, however, as I believed that one day, if we persevered, luck would fall upon us again." Then, on August 12, 2012, the group observed the crucial third event. This time, following the four initial decays, the dubnium-262 (element 105) continued to undergo alpha decays rather than spontaneous fission, transforming into lawrencium-258 (element 103) and then finally mendelevium-254 (element 101). As the chain had been clearly characterized, it demonstrated clearly that element 113 was the source of the decay chain.

On June 8, 2016, the International Union of Pure and Applied Chemists (IUPAC) began a public review of the name and symbol —nihonium and Nh—that the research group proposed to IUPAC. The following is the comment by the group director, Kosuke Morita.

"In the long history of the discovery of chemical elements, we are the first group in Asia to have discovered a new element and then earned naming rights to it. We decided on the name 'nihonium,' bearing in mind the great support we have received from the Japanese people.

Words & Phrases
concrete [kάnkri:t]
3. conclusively [kənklú:sivli]
7. crucial [krú:ʃəl]

Notes
11. mendelevium [mèndəlí:viəm] メンデレビウム
14. the International Union of Pure and Applied Chemists (IUPAC) 国際純正応用化学連合
16. nihonium [ni:hóːniəm] ニホニウム
22. bearing in mind 〜を心に留めておく

UNIT 7

Chemical Elements Periodic Table

	1	2	3	4	5	6	7	8	9
0									
1	₁H								
2	₃Li	₄Be							
3	₁₁Na	₁₂Mg							
4	₁₉K	₂₀Ca	₂₁Sc	₂₂Ti	₂₃V	₂₄Cr	₂₅Mn	₂₆Fe	₂₇Co
5	₃₇Rb	₃₈Sr	₃₉Y	₄₀Zr	₄₁Nb	₄₂Mo	₄₃Tc	₄₄Ru	₄₅Rh
6	₅₅Cs	₅₆Ba	*1	₇₂Hf	₇₃Ta	₇₄W	₇₅Re	₇₆Os	₇₇Ir
7	₈₇Fr	₈₈Ra	*2	₁₀₄Rf	₁₀₅Db	₁₀₆Sg	₁₀₇Bh	₁₀₈Hs	₁₀₉Mt
8	₁₁₉Uue	₁₂₀Ubn	*3	₁₃₈Uto	₁₃₉Ute	₁₄₀Uqn	₁₄₁Uqu	₁₄₂Uqb	₁₄₃Uqt

*1	₅₇La	₅₈Ce	₅₉Pr	₆₀Nd	₆₁Pm	₆₂Sm	₆₃Eu	₆₄Gd
*2	₈₉Ac	₉₀Th	₉₁Pa	₉₂U	₉₃Np	₉₄Pu	₉₅Am	₉₆Cm
*3	₁₂₁Ubu	₁₂₂Ubb	₁₂₃Ubt	₁₂₄Ubq	₁₂₅Ubp	₁₂₆Ubh	₁₂₇Ubs	₁₂₈Ubo

Words & Phrases

1. **approval** [əprúːvəl]
4. **permanent** [pə́ːrmənənt]
5. **gratitude** [grǽtətjùːd]
6. **breakthrough** [bréikθrùː]
7. **tremendously** [triméndəsli]
7. **benefit** [bénəfit]
7. **mankind** [mænkáind]

　　Following the final approval by IUPAC, 'nihonium' and 'Nh' will be added to the periodic table. We are honored to have the name of an element discovered by a research group in Japan earn a permanent seat on the periodic table. We wish to express our deepest gratitude to all those who have given us support over the years. Basic science has produced many breakthroughs which have tremendously benefited mankind in ways unthinkable at the time of the discoveries.

　　It is our hope that seeing the new element discovered in Japan in the periodic table will make people proud and generate

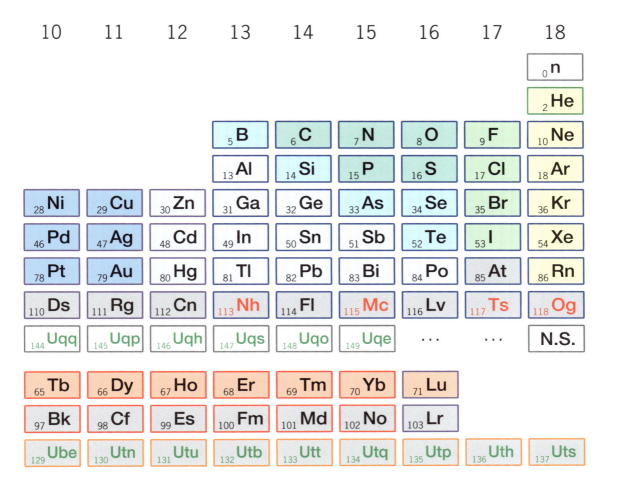

increased interest in science which, in turn will likely lead to a more scientifically-minded general public."

Notes

2. **scientifically-minded**
科学志向の

Post-Reading Activity

Assuming that you find a new element or develop a new product, consider what name you want to give it.

UNIT 7

Comprehension

A Write "T" if the statement is true and write "F" if the statement is false.

1. Superheavy elements have been created in the laboratory and they have less than 103 protons in their nucleus.

2. The work of discovering new superheavy elements is very difficult because the isotopes of 113 produced at RIKEN lasted for more than a hundredth of a second.

3. Although Morita's group could achieve the first two experiments within a year, it took about seven years for the group to observe the crucial third event.

4. Before Morita's group got naming rights of the new element, no researchers in Asian countries had discovered chemical elements.

5. Dr. Morita hopes that the discovery of nihonium will make more people interested in science.

1. (   )   2. (   )   3. (   )   4. (   )   5. (   )

B Fill in the blanks and listen and check your answers.

Researchers at RIKEN have discovered the 113th element which is 1_____ than any of the previously found elements. The purpose of this research was to 2_____ an element with an atomic number of 113, which sounds simple; however, it was actually quite difficult in practice because the 3_____ of producing the target element is extremely small. Researchers around the world are 4_____ to achieve such a discovery. To obtain the 113th element, it was necessary for nuclei to 5_____ with each other 100 trillion times.

Grammar & Vocabulary

A Put the words in the parentheses in the right order.

1. It (that the medicine / been / proved / effective / has not / is) for humans.

2. People (to / a big city / tend / living / lack / in) exercise.

3. The (than / of Japan / is / less / of / population / that) China.

4. This music (who / recommended / like / is / for / those) hip-hop.

5. This substance (of / lead / medicine / to / will / the development).

B Fill in the blank with the appropriate choice.

1. (   ) by a highway police motorcycle, the leading runner turned into Brown Street.
   (a) Lead   (b) Leading
   (c) Led   (d) Having led

2. One gram is equal to (   ) of a kilogram and is approximately 30-times less than an ounce.
   (a) a hundred   (b) a thousand
   (c) a hundredth   (d) a thousandth

3. The classical building, (   ) stands on a hill near a river, is almost a part of natural view.
   (a) which   (b) what
   (c) where   (d) that

4. I would like to stay home (   ) than working outside.
   (a) less   (b) rather
   (c) above   (d) better

5. These solar panels (   ) enough electricity to power around 500 homes.
   (a) attach   (b) install
   (c) absorb   (d) generate

理系論文を読むために

❶ ディスコースマーカー

　Discourse Marker (DM) は，文の展開を示す記号 (sign) のことです。とりわけ科学を扱う文章では文が論理的に構成されているため，DM の使い方をしっかり理解することで「より正確に」読むことができます。また，英文を書く際にも，DM を効果的に利用することで意図した論理を読者に正確に伝えることができます。
　では，品詞や語法に注目しながら，よく使用される DM を見ていきましょう。

❶ 因果関係（原因と結果）

「～が原因で…になった」という関係を明確にします。
　例：大雨だったので，海で泳ぐことができなかった。
　　　　原因　　　　　　結果

ⅰ）接続詞

Because [As / Since] it rained heavily, we couldn't swim in the sea.
It rained yesterday, so we couldn't swim in the sea.

ⅱ）前置詞（句）

Because of [Due to / Owing to / On account of] the heavy rain, we couldn't swim in the sea.

ⅲ）その他

It rained heavily. That is why we couldn't swim in the sea.

❷ 譲歩

「～だけれども，…である」のように「…」の部分を主張し，「譲歩から主張への展開」を表します。
　例：雨が降っていたけれども，彼は海に泳ぎに行った。
　　　→悪条件にもかかわらず「彼が海に泳ぎに行った」ことが強く主張されています。

ⅰ）前置詞（句）

In spite of [Despite] the rain, he went swimming in the sea.

ⅱ）接続詞

Though [Although / Even if] it was raining, he went swimming in the sea.

ⅲ）その他

You may [might] think that he is a genius, but he is not a man of character.
（彼は天才だと思うかもしれないが，人格者ではありません。）

It is true that [Of course / Indeed / Certainly] his theory is famous, but it is fundamentally wrong.
（確かに彼の理論は有名ではあるけれども，根本的に間違っているのです。）

❸ 列挙・手順

序数を有効に用いて手順などを示します。序数のほかに next や then を用いることもあります。

以下は公衆電話の使い方です。

First, [At first, / To start, / The first thing you do is,] pick up the receiver. **Second [Secondly / Then / Next]**, put some coins into the slot. **Then [Next]**, wait for the dial tone. When you hear it, push the number. **Finally, [Lastly, / To finish, / The last thing you do is,]** when you finish, hang up.

hang up：受話器を置く，電話を切る

❹ その他

[対照]　in contrast 対照的に　on the other hand 一方で　while …なのに対して
[例示]　for example [for instance] 例えば　… such as ～ 例えば～のような…
　　　　A is [are] as follows　Aは以下の通りである

✏ Exercise

次のプレゼンテーションの原稿を読んで，文章中のDMの使い方を確認しましょう。また，プレゼンテーションの要約（summary）を日本語で書いてみましょう。

Since aluminum cans are recyclable materials, you should throw away aluminum cans into a recycle bin. You **may not** know this, **but** a large amount of aluminum cans are recycled.

Let me explain how aluminum cans are recycled in my presentation. The recycling process is **as follows**: collection, processing, and recycling.

First of all, used cans which are thrown away must be collected and sorted out into two types: aluminum and steel. **Then**, they are carried to a recycling plant.

Second, in the processing stage, they go through a melting process and turns into melted aluminum. The melted aluminum is **then** made into large blocks called ingots.

Lastly, the rolls are made into aluminum products **such as** cans, wrapped up and ready drink packaging.

Theme / Topic: _____

Summary: _____

Science Lab

3 Gyro Effect
ジャイロ効果

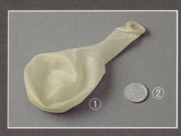

① a rubber balloon (30 cm)
The color should be as faint as possible.
② a 1-yen coin
Any coins will do, but the lighter the better.

Put a coin into a balloon. Blow up the balloon, and tie it at its mouth.

Hold the balloon with both hands, and move it in a circle to make the coin go around inside it.

When the coin starts to go around, stop moving the balloon, and watch how the coin moves.

※ The balloon may break when you blow it up too much or if you do the experiment for a long time.

---

faint
淡い

blow up
膨らませる

tie
結ぶ

huge
巨大な

revolution
公転

axis
軸, 地軸

incline
傾ける

surface
表面

the duration of sunshine
日照時間

positional
位置上の

relation
関係

atmosphere
大気

hemisphere
半球

equator
赤道

Science Lab

📕 **Trivia**

The earth is going around the sun like a huge top as it is rotating (revolution).

The axis of rotation of the earth is inclined at an angle of about 23 degrees to the surface of its revolution.

The axis of rotation of the earth changes little due to the gyro effect. The angle and duration of sunshine upon the earth differs from summer to winter because of the positional relation of the sun and the earth. Seasons on the earth come out of the difference of the atmosphere's warming in summer and winter.

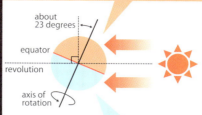

Summer in the northern hemisphere
The atmosphere is easily warmed up because the sun shines longer from more directly above.

Winter in the southern hemisphere
The atmosphere is hardly warmed up because the sun shines shorter from a lower angle.

4 Vibration Control Structure
耐震と制震

cardboard
厚紙

glue
のり

five-story tower
五重塔

ancient
昔の

construction
建造物

suppression
抑制

pendulum
振り子

suppress
抑える

wisdom
知恵

peculiar
特有の

brace
支柱

sideways
横に

Preparation

① a sheet of paper as thick as drawing paper (B4 size and over)
② a sheet of strong cardboard (about A4 size)
③ a paper clip, a ruler, a pencil, a cutter knife, and glue

Trivia

Five-story towers are ancient Japanese constructions with earthquake suppression.

Many five-story towers in temples have an earthquake suppression system using ancient Japanese construction technology. The five-story tower of Horyuji, the world-oldest wooden temple located in Nara Prefecture, has a central column fixed only at the top of the tower, which works as a pendulum to suppress shaking. This idea is also used in Tokyo Skytree. That is ancient wisdom which is peculiar to Japan, an earthquake country.

Science Lab

 **Procedure**

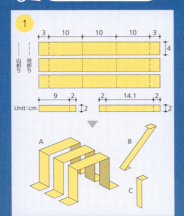

1. Cut out paper in the size shown, and fold along the dotted line.

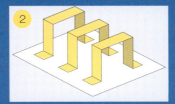

2. Attach A on cardboard at about 5 cm intervals, and line up three of these stands.

3. Put B (brace) on the middle stand.

4. Put C (pendulum) on the front stand in the middle of the underside of the top, and put a paper clip at the bottom.

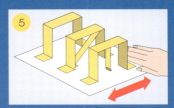

5. Move the stands sideways, and watch how the frame moves.

Presentation
プレゼンテーションをしよう

プレゼンテーションでは，内容を聞き手にわかりやすく効果的に伝えることがとても大事です。ときには，専門知識をもたない人にプレゼンテーションをしなくてはならないこともあるかもしれません。ここでは，特に科学者や技術者が気をつけたいプレゼンテーションのコツを見ていきましょう。

❶ **Check** your audience. Who are you presenting to?

　　プレゼンテーションをする相手は誰でしょうか。プレゼンテーションをする分野についてよく知っている人なのか，年齢層はどうなのか，など聞き手によって話す内容や用意する資料も変わってきます。

❷ **Connect** with the audience. Show them your presentation matters to them.

　　発表する内容が聞き手にとって，知っておくべきことだと思ってもらうことが大事です。それができれば，聞き手の興味がぐっと高まり，しっかりプレゼンテーションを聞いてもらえます。

❸ **Use** analogies. Give examples everyone can understand.

　　プレゼンテーションの内容が難しいという印象をもたれてしまってはいけません。聞き手にとって，身近な例を示して説明しましょう。難しいことでも，多くの例え話を交えることで理解しやすくなります。

❹ **Pick** numbers that are meaningful to your audience.

　　ものの大きさや重さ，実験で明らかになった数値などは大事ですが，その数字がどれほど意味があるのかを聞き手にしっかり伝えましょう。いたずらに数字を伝えるのではなく，本当に必要な情報だけを言いましょう。

❺ **Use** less text and **more** visuals.

　　ビジュアルエイドはプレゼンテーションには欠かせません。スライドを使って発表する場合は，メインアイディアを箇条書きしたスライドよりも，イラストや写真，グラフをメインとして，要となる文やフレーズを添えたスライドの方が聞き手の記憶に残ります。

❻ **Deliver** with passion and enthusiasm.

　　プレゼンテーションをするときは自信をもって，大きな声ではっきりと話しましょう。また，聞き手とアイコンタクトをとりましょう。

Useful Expressions

Introducing the topic
I'm going to talk about…
My topic today is…

Overview (outline of presentation)
First of all, I'll…
… and then I'll go on to…
Then [Next]…
Finally [Lastly]…

Finishing a section
That's all I have to say about…
So much for…

Starting a new section
Let's turn now to…
The next issue [topic/area] I'd like to focus on…
I'd like to expand [elaborate] on…
Now we'll move on to…

Analyzing a point and giving recommendations
Let's consider this in more detail…
What does this mean for…?
Why is this important?
A good example of this is…
To give you an example, …

Summarizing and concluding
To sum up…
Let's summarize briefly what we've looked at…
If I can just sum up the main points…
Finally, let me remind you of some of the issues we've covered…
In conclusion…
In short…

Paraphrasing and clarifying
In other words…
So what I'm saying is…
To put it more simply…
Does anyone have any questions or comments?
Any questions?

Exercise

実験レポートをもとにプレゼンテーションをしてみましょう。

CHECK　　　　　　　　　発表者：＿＿＿＿＿＿＿＿＿＿＿＿＿＿＿＿

☐ 聞き手を意識したプレゼンテーションをしている。
☐ 発表する内容について興味をもたせる努力をしている。
☐ 例えなどを使って，わかりやすく説明している。
☐ 効果的なビジュアルエイドを多用している。
☐ 大きな声ではっきり話している。
☐ アイコンタクトをとっている。

◆発展

あなたが開発した商品を，専門知識のない会社の経営陣にプレゼンテーションをしてみましょう。

理系論文を読むために

❷ 統計の読み取り方

科学系分野では，実験や観察の結果をグラフや図で表現し，それを英語で説明する場面が多くあります。次の例を参考に，グラフの内容を説明する上で必要となる英語の表現を学びましょう。

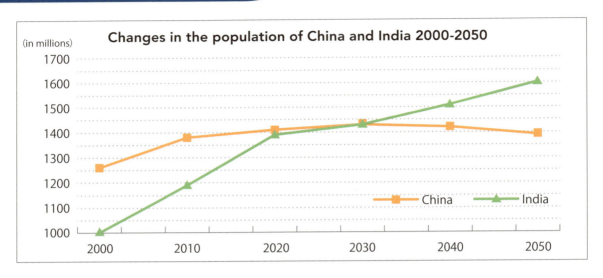

❶ 上のグラフの内容を説明するために，まず大まかなアウトラインを決めます。

ⅰ) イントロ：トピックについて

Population growth in China and India

ⅱ) 本論1：Chinaの場合

- 2000-2030: steadily increase and reach the peak in 2030
- 2030-2050: fall to 1.4 billion

ⅲ) 本論2：Indiaの場合

- 2000-2030: rapidly increase and overtake China in 2030
- 2030-2050: continue to increase

ⅳ) 全体のまとめ

- What is major difference between the two countries?
- after 2030: the population of China will fall but that of India will rise

❷ アウトラインに沿って，文章をまとめます。

　The graph shows changes of population in China and India from the year 2000 to 2050.
ⅰ)

　In China, the population was about 1.5 billion and the number **is predicted** to **rise steadily** to 1.45 billion by 2030. The population will **reach its peak in** 2030 and will be about 1.45 billion. However, it is expected to **decrease slowly** to about 1.4 billion in 2050.
ⅱ)

　In contrast, although the population in India is about one billion in 2000, it will have increased rapidly to about 1.45 billion in 2030, when India will overtake China. The population is expected to rise after 2030.
ⅲ)

　Overall, the major difference between the two countries is that after 2030 the population of China will fall **whereas** that of India will continue to rise.
ⅳ)

 Useful Expressions

【増加】rise / go up / increase / grow / soar
【減少】fall / drop / decrease / sink / go down
【最大・最小】reach a peak / fell to a low / sink to a trough / reach a bottom
【変化なし】remain steady [constant / stable] / is unchanged / do not change / stabilized

The number started to **increase** [**go up** / **rise**] in 2000. (増加)
    (rise **quickly** [**rapidly**] / increase **by** [**to**] 10 %)
          by 10% 10%増加, to 10% 10%に増加
The number will **decrease** [**go down** / **fall** / **drop**] in 2030. (減少)
    (drop **slightly** [**steadily** / **slowly** / **gradually**])
The number of India will be **higher than** that of India in 2050. (比較)
    (**approximately** [**almost** / **about**] **the same**)
In contrast [**By contrast**], China will decrease its population after 2030. (対比)
It is **estimated** that the population of China will be about 1.45 billion in 2030. (予測・見込み)

✎ Exercise

次のグラフの内容を説明してみましょう。( )内に入る語句を下の Word Bank から選びましょう。

The graph shows (　　　) over the course of a day.

The busiest time of the day is in (　　　). There is a (　　　) increase between (　　　) and (　　　). After this the number (　　　) (　　　) to less than 2000 at 10 o'clock.

Between 11 a.m. and 3 p.m. the number remains (　　　). In the afternoon, the number reaches a (　　　) at 6 p.m. After 6 p.m., number (　　　) significantly and it starts to (　　　) slightly at 7 p.m. But from 8 p.m. it (　　　).

(　　　), the graph shows the station is most crowded in (　　　) and (　　　) periods.

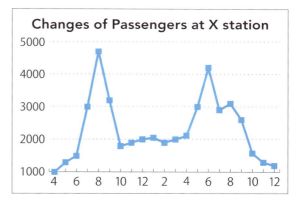

Changes of Passengers at X station

> **Word Bank**
> 8 a.m. / the early morning / sharp / quickly / changes of passengers at X station / drops / 6 a.m. / steady / falls / increase / early evening / overall / the morning / continues to decrease / peak

UNIT 8 Truth, Beauty, and Other Scientific Misconceptions

Many scientists strive to find the elegant theories they often find most compelling. Despite the value many scientists place on elegance, they can have divergent notions about "what is simple and beautiful." Lisa Randall, one of the most influential theoretical physicists, expounds her insights in the understanding of theoretical particle physics in her book.

Pre-Reading Activity

Part 1

Many of you like physics. Some say that it is great to enjoy tackling physical questions using mathematical formulas. Others say that they love to observe physical phenomena. Why do you think people are interested in physics? Share your idea with your friends.

Words & Phrases

misconception
[mìskənsépʃən]

strive
[straiv]

compelling
[kəmpéliŋ]

divergent
[divə́ːrdʒənt]

expound
[ikspáund]

particle
[páːrtikl]

In February 2007, the Nobel Prize–winning theoretical physicist Murray Gell-Mann spoke at the elite TED conference in California, where innovators working in science, technology, literature, entertainment, and other cutting edge domains gather once a year to present new developments and insights about a wide variety of subjects. Murray's crowd-pleasing talk, which was rewarded with a standing ovation, was on the topic of truth and beauty in science. The basic premise of the talk can best be summarized with his words, which echo those of John Keats: "Truth

Truth, Beauty, and Other Scientific Misconceptions

is beauty and beauty is truth."

Gell-Mann had good reasons to believe his grand statement. He had made some of his most significant Nobel Prize–winning discoveries about quarks by searching for an underlying principle that could elegantly organize the seemingly random set of data that experiments had discovered in the 1960s. In Murray's experience, the search for beauty—or at least simplicity—had also led to truth.

Here is part of his speech.

I used to work in this field of elementary particles. What happens to matter if you chop it up very fine? What is it made of? The laws of these particles are valid throughout the universe, and they're very much connected with the history of the universe.

We know a lot about four forces. There must be a lot more, but those are at very, very small distances, and we haven't really interacted with them very much yet. The main thing I want to talk about is this: that we have this remarkable experience in this field of fundamental physics and that beauty is a very successful criterion for choosing the right theory. Why on earth could that be so?

Post-Reading Activity

Murray Gell-Mann is a physicist awarded with Nobel Prize. What did he achieve? What did he stress in the presentation he made at the TED conference in California in 2007? Do you like his idea? How about your friends? Ask your friends if they like his idea.

UNIT 8

Pre-Reading Activity  Part 2

In his presentation, Murray Gell-Mann refers to a man he admires, Albert Einstein. His picture is put next to the screen over the stage, and on the screen the audience can see the following slide. Do you know Albert Einstein? What is he famous for?

Elementary particles are the building blocks of all matter everywhere in the universe. Their properties are connected with the fundamental forces of nature. We are very familiar through observation with four such forces:

Gravitation
Electromagnetism
The Strong Force, which holds atomic nuclei together
The Weak Force, responsible for several forms of radioactivity

Words & Phrases
1. **gravitation** [ɡrævətéiʃən]
2. **confident** [kánfədənt]
3. **definitely** [défənitli]
3. **encourage** [inkə́:ridʒ]
6. **fairly** [féərli]
8. **put forward**
8. **partially** [pá:rʃəli]
9. **disagreement** [dìsəɡrí:mənt]
12. **figure** [fíɡjər]

Notes
Albert Einstein
[ǽlbərt áinstain]
(1879-1955)
米国の理論物理学者

Murray Gell-Mann continues his speech. He sounds very confident of his belief in science. He recalls what Albert Einstein said to him. His words definitely encouraged Gell-Mann. What did Einstein say to him?

Well, here's an example from my own experience. It's fairly dramatic, actually, to have this happen. Three or four of us, in 1957, put forward a partially complete theory of one of these forces, the weak force. And it was in disagreement with seven— seven, count them, seven experiments. The experiments were all wrong.

And we published before knowing that, because we figured it was so beautiful, it's gotta be right! The experiments had to be wrong, and they were. Now our friend over there, Albert Einstein,

Truth, Beauty, and Other Scientific Misconceptions

used to pay very little attention when people said, "You know, there's a man with an experiment that seems to disagree with special relativity. DC Miller. What about that?" And he would say, "Aw, that'll go away." (Laughter)

Now, why does stuff like that work? That's the question. Now, yeah, what do we mean by beautiful? That's one thing. I'll try to make that clear—partially clear. Why should it work, and is this something to do with human beings? I'll let you in on the answer to the last one that I offer, and that is, it has nothing to do with human beings.

And someday, we may actually figure out the fundamental unified theory of the particles and forces, what I call the "fundamental law." We may not even be terribly far from it. But even if we don't run across it in our lifetimes, we can still think there is one out there, and we're just trying to get closer and closer to it. I think that's the main point to be made. We express these things mathematically. And when the mathematics is very simple—when in terms of some mathematical notation, you can write the theory in a very brief space, without a lot of complication—that's essentially what we mean by beauty or elegance.

---

p.86
Notes

electromagnetism
[ilèktroumǽgnətizm]
電磁気

nuclei
[njúːkliái]
核 (nucleusの複数形)

radioactivity
[rèidiouæktívəti]
放射能

9. **weak force**
弱い力

p.87
Words & Phrases

11. **figure out**
13. **terribly**
[térəbli]
14. **run across ~**
18. **in terms of ~**
18. **notation**
[noutéiʃən]
19. **complication**
[kàmpləkéiʃən]
20. **essentially**
[isénʃəli]

Notes

3. **special relativity**
[spéʃəl relətívəti]
特殊相対性理論

3. **DC Miller**
[díːsíː mílər]
(1886-1941) 米国の物理学者

Post-Reading Activity

Murray Gell-Mann talks about one example from his experience. He says it's fairly dramatic. How dramatic is it?

According to Gell-Mann, the "fundamental law" exists, and even if we don't run across it in our lifetimes, we can still think there is one out there, and we're just trying to get closer and closer to it. What do you think leads him to this belief? Exchange your ideas with your friends.

UNIT 8

Pre-Reading Activity

Murray Gell-Mann's enthusiastic presentation captivated the audience. Lisa Randall, however, as a physicist, doesn't agree with what he meant by beauty or elegance, as you can see later in Part 3. Why do you think she is skeptical about what Gell-Mann claimed?

Words & Phrases

enthusiastic [inθùːziǽstik]
captivate [kǽptəvèit]
skeptical [sképtikəl]
1. dispute [dispjúːt]
3. more often than not
3. reveal [rivíːl]
4. confess [kənfés]
4. assumption [əsʌ́mpʃən]
4. slippery [slípəri]
7. aesthetically [esθétikəli]
7. satisfying [sǽtisfàiiŋ]
7. subjective [səbdʒéktiv]
8. reliable [riláiəbl]
8. arbiter [áːrbətər]
9. identification [aidèntəfikéiʃən]
11. equivalent [ikwívələnt]
13. specifically [spisífikəli]
15. sentiment [séntəmənt]
18. to make matters ~
19. disconcerting [dìskənsə́ːrtiŋ]

No one in the audience disputed his claim. After all, most people love the idea that beauty and truth go together and that the search for one will more often than not reveal the other. But I confess that I have always found this assumption a little slippery. Although everyone would love to believe that beauty is at the heart 5 of great scientific theories, and that the truth will always be aesthetically satisfying, beauty is at least in part a subjective criterion that will never be a reliable arbiter of truth.

The basic problem with the identification of truth and beauty is that it does not always hold—it holds only when it does. If truth 10 and beauty were equivalent, the words "ugly truth" would never have entered our vocabulary. Even though those words weren't specifically directed toward science, observations about the world are not always beautiful. Darwin's colleague Thomas Huxley nicely summarized this sentiment when he said "science is 15 organized common sense where many a beautiful theory was killed by an ugly fact."

To make matters more difficult, physicists have to allow for the disconcerting observation that the universe and its elements are not entirely beautiful. We observe a plethora of messy phenomena 20 and a zoo of particles that we'd like to understand. Ideally, physicists would love to find a simple theory capable of explaining all such observations that uses only a spare set of rules and the fewest possible fundamental ingredients. But even when searching for a simple, elegant, unifying theory—one that can be used to predict the result of any particle physics experiment—we know that even if we find it, we would need many further steps to connect it to our world.

5   The universe is complex. New ingredients and principles are generally needed before we can connect a simple, spare formulation to the more complicated surrounding world. Those additional ingredients might destroy the beauty present in the initial proposed formulation, much as earmarks all too often interfere with a
10 congressional bill's initial idealistic intentions. Given the potential pitfalls; how do we go about trying to go beyond what we know? How do we try to interpret as-yet-unexplained phenomena?

p.88
Words & Phrases

20. **plethora** [pléθərə]
20. **messy** [mési]
21. **ideally** [aidí:əli]
23. **spare** [speər]
24. **ingredient** [ingrí:diənt]

Notes

14. **Charles Darwin** [tʃá:rlz dá:rwin] (1809-1882) 英国の自然科学者
14. **Thomas Huxley** [táməs háksli] (1825-1895) 英国の生物学者
21. **zoo of particle** 新種の素粒子群

p.89
Words & Phrases

2. **predict** [pridíkt]
5. **complex** [kəmpléks]
6. **formulation** [fɔ:rmjuléiʃən]
7. **surrounding** [səráundiŋ]
9. **earmark** [íərmà:rk]
9. **interfere** [ìntərfíər]
10. **congressional** [kəŋgréʃənl]
11. **pitfall** [pítfɔ:l]

Post-Reading Activity

Lisa Randall disagrees with Gell-Mann's idea of beauty and the role of aesthetic criteria in science. Briefly list two arguments that form the base of her viewpoint.

Do you agree with her viewpoint? Ask your friends if they agree or not. If someone has a different opinion from yours, ask him or her why and discuss where you agree and disagree after your talk.

UNIT 8

Comprehension

A Write "T" if the statement is true and write "F" if the statement is false.

1. Albert Einstein didn't show any interest in the result of DC Miller's experiment.
2. Murray Gell-Mann said, "Truth is beauty and beauty is truth."
3. Lisa Randall completely disagrees with Gell-Mann's idea of beauty and truth in science.
4. Lisa Randall sympathizes with Thomas Huxley's sentiment mentioned above.
5. Lisa Randall thinks that beauty has nothing to do with science.

1. ( )   2. ( )   3. ( )   4. ( )   5. ( )

B Which word do you think best describes Murray Gell-Mann as a scientist? Add reasons why you think so.

(a) enthusiastic   (b) critical   (c) imaginative   (d) reserved
(e) confident   (f) positive   (g) optimistic   (h) negative

....

....

....

C Which word do you think best describes Lisa Randall as a scientist? Add reasons why you think so.

(a) enthusiastic   (b) critical   (c) imaginative   (d) reserved
(e) confident   (f) positive   (g) optimistic   (h) negative

....

....

....

D Compare the two physicists, Murray Gell-Mann and Lisa Randall, and discuss which one is more qualified as a scientist.

Expand Your Vocabulary

▶ 単語を覚えたら☑。赤フィルターを使えば効率アップ。

Chemistry

A
- acceleration 名 促進
- acceptor 名 受容体
- acid 名 酸
- acidic 形 酸性の
- activator 名 活性化剤
- addition reaction 名 付加反応
- additive 名 添加剤
- adhesive 名 接着剤
- affinity 名 親和力
- agent 名 試薬, 薬品
- agitation 名 撹拌
- allotrope 名 同素体
- anion 名 陰イオン → cation
- anode 名 (電解槽の)陽極, (蓄電池の)陰極 → cathode
- aqueous solution 名 水溶液
- aromatic compound 名 芳香族化合物
- atomic number 名 原子番号
- atomic weight 名 原子量

B
- base 名 塩基
- basic 形 塩基性の
- buffer 名 緩衝
- buffer solution 名 緩衝溶液

C
- catalyst 名 触媒
- cathode 名 (蓄電池の)陽極, (電解槽の)陰極 → anode
- cation 名 陽イオン → anion
- centrifugation 名 遠心分離
- chain reaction 名 連鎖反応
- chemical bond 名 化学結合
- chemical equation 名 化学方程式
- chemical formula 名 化学式
- chemical(s) 名 化学薬品[物質]
- chloride 名 塩化物
- chlorine 名 塩素
- chromosome 名 染色体
- colligative property 名 束一的性質
- combustion 名 燃焼
- compound (s) 名 混合物, 化合物
- concentration 名 濃縮, 濃度
- condensation 名 凝縮
- conjugate 名 動 共役(させる)
- contamination 名 汚染
- coordinate bond 名 配位結合
- corrosion 名 浸食, 腐食
- covalent bond 名 共有結合
- culture 名 動 培養(する)

D
- decomposition 名 分解
- density 名 密度, 濃度
- deposit 名 沈殿物
- detergent 名 洗浄剤
- diffusion 名 拡散
- dipole 名 双極子
- dissolution [dissolving] 名 溶解
- distillation 名 蒸留
- distilled water 名 蒸留水
- DNA (Deoxyribonucleic Acid) DNA[デオキシリボ核酸]
- double bond 名 二重結合
- ductility 名 展延性, 伸度

E
- efflorescence 名 風解, 風化
- effusion 名 浸出, 流出
- electric dissociation 名 電離
- electro motive force 名 起電力
- electrode 名 電極
- electrolysis 名 電気分解, 電解
- electrolyte 名 電解質, 電解液
- electron affinity 名 電子親和力
- electrostatic 形 静電の
- element 名 元素
- empirical formula 名 実験式
- endothermic 形 吸熱の
- endothermic reaction 名 吸熱反応
- enzyme 名 酵素
- equilibrium 名 平衡
- evaporation 名 蒸発
- exothermic 形 発熱の
- expansion 名 膨張
- extraction 名 抽出

F
- fermentation 名 発酵
- filtration 名 濾過
- flame reaction 名 炎色反応
- fractional distillation 名 分留
- free electron 名 自由電子
- freezing point 名 氷点, 凝固点
- functional group 名 官能基
- fusion 名 溶融, 融解

G
- gas constant 名 気体定数
- gene 名 遺伝子
- genetic recombination 名 遺伝子組み換え
- gravimetric analysis 名 重量分析

H
- half-life 名 半減期
- heat of formation 名 生成熱
- heat of fusion 名 融解熱
- heat of reaction 名 反応熱
- heat of solidification 名 凝固熱
- homogeneity 名 均一(性)
- hybrid 名 形 混成(の)
- hydration 名 水和
- hydrolysis 名 加水分解

I
- incubator 名 定温器
- infrared radiation 名 赤外線
- intermolecular force 名 分子間力
- intramolecular 名 分子内の

Expand Your Vocabulary (Physics)

- ion(ic) bond 名 イオン結合
- ionization 名 電離, イオン化
- isomer 名 異性体
- isotope 名 同位元素, 同位体

K
- kinetic energy 名 運動エネルギー
- kinetics 名 動力学, 速度論

L
- liquid crystal 名 液晶
- lubricant 名 潤滑剤

M
- macromolecule 名 高分子
- mass number 名 質量数
- melting point 名 融点
- mess flask 名 メスフラスコ
- molality 名 重量モル濃度
- molecular structure 名 分子構造

N
- neutralization 名 中和
- neutron 名 中性子
- nuclear fission 名 核分裂
- nuclear fusion 名 核融合

O
- osmotic pressure 名 浸透圧
- oxidation [oxide] 名 酸化作用 [物]

P
- pertial pressure 名 分圧
- periodic table 名 周期表
- permeation 名 浸透, 透過
- photon 名 光子
- pigment 名 色素
- polymer 名 高分子, 重合体
- polymerization 名 重合

Q
- quantum mechanics 名 量子力学

R
- radiation 名 放射線
- radioactivity 名 放射能
- rare earth element 名 希土類元素
- rare gas 名 希ガス
- reactant 名 反応物
- redox 名 酸化還元
- reduction 名 還元
- refractive index 名 屈折率
- resonance effect 名 共鳴効果
- reversible reaction 名 可逆反応

S
- saturation 名 飽和
- solidification 名 凝固, 固化
- solubility 名 溶解度
- solution 名 溶液
- solvent 名 溶媒
- specific gravity 名 比重
- sublimation 名 昇華
- sulfuric acid 名 硫酸
- super alloy 名 超合金
- supersonic wave 名 超音波
- surface tension 名 表面張力
- surfactant 名 界面活性物質 [剤]
- synergism 名 相乗作用

T
- test tube 名 試験管
- thermodynamics 名 熱力学
- thermoplastic 名 熱可塑性
- tissue 名 組織
- titration 名 滴定
- toxicity 名 毒性

V
- valence electron 名 価電子
- vapor pressure 名 蒸気圧
- visible light [rays] 名 可視光

W
- weak acid 名 弱酸

X
- X-ray 名 X線

Z
- zwitter ion 名 双 [両] 性イオン

Physics

A
- accelerate 動 加速する
- action 名 作用
- alternating current 名 交流
- angular frequency 名 角振動数
- angular velocity 名 角速度
- atmospheric pressure 名 大気圧

B
- buoyance 名 浮力

C
- cathode ray 名 陰極線
- centrifugal force 名 遠心力
- charge 名 電荷
- circuit 名 回路
- collision 名 衝突
- combustion 名 燃焼
- component of force 名 分力
- conductor 名 導体
- couple 名 偶力

D
- decay 名 崩壊
- deflect 動 （光の）方向を変える
- dielectric polarization 名 誘電分極
- dielectrics 名 誘電体
- diffract 動 回折する
- direct current 名 直流
- discharge 名 放電
- drag 名 抗力

E
- earth 名 接地
- elastic force 名 弾性力
- electric capacity 名 電気容量
- electric current 名 電流
- electric field 名 電場 [界]
- electric potential difference 名 電位差

Expand Your Vocabulary (Mechanical Engineering)

- electric resistance 名 電気抵抗
- electrical field 名 電場[界]
- electrolysis 名 電気分解
- electrolyte 名 電解質
- electromagnetic induction 名 電磁誘導
- electromagnetic wave 名 電磁波
- electrostatic force 名 静電力
- electrostatic induction 名 静電誘導
- equilibrium 名 平衡
- excited state 名 励起状態
- expansion 名 膨張

F
- fission 名 分裂
- free electron 名 自由電子
- frequency 名 周波数, 振動数
- friction 名 摩擦

G
- gravity 名 重力, 引力

I
- impulse 名 力積, 衝撃
- induced current 名 誘導電流
- induced electromotive force 名 誘導起電力
- inertia 名 慣性
- insulator 名 絶縁体
- interfere 動 干渉する
- irradiate 動 照射する

K
- kinetic energy 名 運動エネルギー

L
- law of mass conservation 名 質量保存の法則
- line of magnetic force 名 磁力線

M
- magnetic field 名 磁場[界]
- magnetic flux 名 磁束
- magnetic force 名 磁力
- mass 名 質量
- mass number 名 質量数
- material particle 名 質点
- melting point 名 融点
- molecule 名 分子
- momentum 名 運動量
- mutual inductance [induction] 名 相互誘導

N
- nucleus 名 原子核

P
- parallel 名 平衡
- phase 名 位相
- photoelectric effect 名 光電効果
- photoelectrons 名 光電子
- polarization 名 分極
- potential energy 名 位置エネルギー
- projection 名 投射

Q
- quantity of electricity 名 電気量
- quantum condition 名 量子条件
- quantum number 名 量子数

R
- radiation 名 放射線
- reaction 名 反作用
- rectilinear movement 名 直進
- refraction 名 屈折
- repel 動 反発する
- resistance 名 抵抗
- resolution 名 分解
- resonate 動 共振[共鳴]する
- resultant force 名 合力

S
- self-induction 名 自己誘導
- semiconductor 名 半導体
- series 名 直列
- specific heat 名 比熱
- specific resistance 名 比抵抗
- spectrum 名 スペクトラム, スペクトル
- standing wave 名 定常波

T
- the center of gravity 名 重心
- thermal efficiency 名 熱効率
- thermal electron 名 熱電子
- total reflection 名 全反射

V
- vacuum discharge 名 真空放電
- virtual image 名 虚像
- voltage 名 電圧
- voltmeter 名 電圧計

W
- water pressure 名 水圧
- wave length 名 波長

Mechanical Engineering

A
- abrasive 名 研磨剤
- abutment 名 橋台
- acceleration 名 加速(度)
- accurate 形 詳しい
- acetate 名 酢酸塩
- adhesion 名 接着
- adhesive 名 粘着剤
- alloy 名 合金
- alternator 名 交流発電機
- altitude 名 高度
- analysis 名 解析, 分析
- angle 名 角, アングル材
- appliance 名 器具, 装置
- arch 名 迫持(せりもち)

Expand Your Vocabulary (Mechanical Engineering)

- [ ] assembly 名 組み立て部品
- [ ] axle 名 (車)軸

B
- [ ] balance 名 てんびん, つり合い
- [ ] bearing 名 軸受け
- [ ] brace 名 締め金
- [ ] breeder reactor 名 増殖炉

C
- [ ] cell 名 セル[単電池]
- [ ] charger 名 荷電器, チャージャー
- [ ] chemical engineering 名 化学工業
- [ ] chrome 名 クロム鋼
- [ ] chuck 動 名 つかむ; くわえ
- [ ] clamp 名 かすがい
- [ ] combustion 名 燃焼
- [ ] component 名 構成部品
- [ ] compress 動 圧縮する
- [ ] compressor 名 圧縮機
- [ ] conduction 名 伝導
- [ ] constant 名 定数
- [ ] contraption 名 (変わった)仕掛け, 装置
- [ ] conversion 名 転換, 変換
- [ ] corrosion 名 腐食
- [ ] coulomb 名 クーロン(電気量の単位)
- [ ] coupling 名 継ぎ手, 結合
- [ ] curves 名 曲線定規

D
- [ ] defective 名 不良品
- [ ] deform 動 歪める
- [ ] degree 名 平面角の単位
- [ ] depth 名 見こみ, 歯たけ
- [ ] diagram 名 線図, 図形, 図表
- [ ] dimension 名 大きさ, 外形寸法
- [ ] distribution 名 分布, 流通, 配分
- [ ] dynamics 名 力学

E
- [ ] elastic 形 伸縮性の, 弾力がある
- [ ] electrode 名 電極
- [ ] emulsion 名 乳剤
- [ ] enthalpy 名 全熱量, エンタルピ
- [ ] excavation 名 掘削

F
- [ ] fail 名 故障
- [ ] failure 名 操作ミス, 破損
- [ ] fiber 名 繊維
- [ ] fluid 名 液体
- [ ] flywheel 名 弾み車
- [ ] fraction 名 分数
- [ ] friction 名 摩擦
- [ ] fuel 名 燃料, フュエル

G
- [ ] gauge 名 口径
- [ ] gear 名 歯車, 伝動装置
- [ ] generate 動 発生させる, 生み出す
- [ ] generator 名 ダイナモ, 発電機

H
- [ ] horizontal 形 横(軸)
- [ ] hydraulics 名 水力学

I
- [ ] impedance 名 電気抵抗
- [ ] ingot 名 地金

J
- [ ] joint 名 接合箇所継ぎ目

K
- [ ] kinetics 名 力学

L
- [ ] load 名 積荷, 積載量
- [ ] lumber [timber] 名 材木

M
- [ ] management 名 管理, マネジメント
- [ ] manometer 名 圧力計
- [ ] manufacturing 名 製造, 生産
- [ ] mean (value) 名 平均(値)
- [ ] mechanize 動 機械化する
- [ ] modular 形 規準寸法の, 組み立てユニットによる
- [ ] mold 名 型
- [ ] motion 名 動き, 動作, 運動

N
- [ ] norm 名 規範

O
- [ ] oscilloscope 名 オシロスコープ, 信号電圧波型観測装置
- [ ] outage 名 動作不能状態
- [ ] oxidation 名 酸化

P
- [ ] pivot 名 遊動軸, ピボット
- [ ] plunger 名 棒ピストン
- [ ] plywood 名 合板
- [ ] polygon 名 多角形
- [ ] power plant 名 原動機, 発電装置
- [ ] precise 形 詳しい
- [ ] proportion 名 割合
- [ ] PWR (Pressurized-Water Reactor) 名 加圧水型原子炉

R
- [ ] radiate 動 放出する, 放射状にのびる
- [ ] refine 動 精製する, リファイン
- [ ] rivet 名 鋲
- [ ] rotating shaft 名 軸

S
- [ ] scheme 名 組織
- [ ] screwdriver 名 ねじまわし
- [ ] short circuit 名 短絡, ショート
- [ ] silicone polymer 名 シリコーンポリマ(ケイ素化合物重合体)
- [ ] stability 名 安定性
- [ ] statics 名 静力学
- [ ] superstructure 名 上部構造, 船楼
- [ ] suspension 名 懸濁液, サスペンション

T
- [ ] tension 名 緊張
- [ ] torque 名 回転力, トルク
- [ ] transmission 名 変速装置, トランスミッション
- [ ] turbine 名 タービン, 羽根車

V
- [ ] vertical 形 垂直の, 立軸の
- [ ] vise 名 万力
- [ ] voltage 名 起電力
- [ ] volume 名 容積

W
- [ ] weld 名 動 溶接(する)

Expand Your Vocabulary (Electrical / Electronic Engineering)

Electrical / Electronic Engineering

A
- [ ] AC (Alternating Current) 名 交流
- [ ] accumulator 名 累算器
- [ ] alternate 名 代理, 交代
- [ ] altimeter 名 高度測量器
- [ ] ammeter 名 電流計
- [ ] amplifier 名 平衡[二極]増幅器
- [ ] anodize 動 陽極化する
- [ ] arc 名 電弧, アーク

B
- [ ] ballast 名 安定器, バラスト
- [ ] binary 形 二進の
- [ ] blackout 名 停電
- [ ] branch 名 分枝, 分岐, 二又
- [ ] brownout 名 節電
- [ ] bulb 名 電球

C
- [ ] cable 名 電線, ケーブル
- [ ] circuit 名 回路
- [ ] circuit diagram 名 回路図
- [ ] coaxial 形 同軸の, 同ケーブルの
- [ ] coil 名 線輪, コイル
- [ ] commutator 名 電流転換器, 整流子
- [ ] condenser 名 蓄電池, コンデンサー
- [ ] conductor 名 電導体
- [ ] connection 名 連結, 接続
- [ ] connector 名 接続器, コネクタ
- [ ] coulomb 名 クーロン（電気量の単位）
- [ ] couple 名 電対
- [ ] current 名 電流計
- [ ] cycle 名 周波

D
- [ ] DC (Direct Current) 名 直流
- [ ] density 名 密度
- [ ] device 名 装置
- [ ] dimmer 名 調光器
- [ ] discharge 動 放電する
- [ ] distort 動 （音や画質を）ひずませる
- [ ] duration 名 持続(期)

E
- [ ] electrical outlet 名 差込口
- [ ] electrician 名 電気技師
- [ ] electrify 動 電化する, 帯電する
- [ ] electrode 名 電極棒
- [ ] electrolysis 名 電気分解
- [ ] electromagnet 名 電気磁石
- [ ] electromagnetism 名 電磁気(学)
- [ ] electrostatic 形 静電の
- [ ] excessive 形 過剰な

F
- [ ] farad 名 ファラド（静電容量の単位）
- [ ] filament 名 （電球・真空管の）フィラメント, （白熱）繊条
- [ ] flick 動 （スイッチなどを）パチッとつける
- [ ] flux 名 フラックス（はんだづけ用の溶剤）

G
- [ ] galvanometer 名 （微量な電流の流れを計る）検流計
- [ ] gamma ray 名 ガンマ線
- [ ] generate 動 （電気を）発生させる, おこす
- [ ] glitch 名 電力の突然の異常
- [ ] grid 名 送電網, （電線などの）敷設網

H
- [ ] high-voltage 名 高電圧
- [ ] homing 形 自動追尾の
- [ ] humidistat 名 調湿器
- [ ] hydroelectric 形 水力発電の
- [ ] hydropower 名 水力式, 水力

I
- [ ] impede 動 阻害する, 妨げる
- [ ] impulse 名 衝撃, インパルス
- [ ] incandescent 形 白熱の, 白熱光を発する
- [ ] induced current 名 誘導電流
- [ ] induction 名 誘導, 感応
- [ ] inductor 名 誘導子
- [ ] infrared 名 形 赤外線（の）
- [ ] installation 名 設置, 取りつけ
- [ ] insulate 動 （電気を）絶縁する
- [ ] insulation 名 絶縁体
- [ ] integrate 動 統合する
- [ ] intensity 名 （光・熱などが）強烈
- [ ] interaction 名 相互作用
- [ ] interference 名 （電波などの）妨害, 干渉

J
- [ ] jack 名 ジャック（プラグの差込口）

K
- [ ] knob 名 （電気器具の）つまみ, ノブ

L
- [ ] LCD (Liquid Crystal Display) 名 液晶表示装置
- [ ] lineman 名 架線工夫
- [ ] loadstone 名 天然磁石
- [ ] logic gate 名 論理ゲート（論理演算を行う回路）
- [ ] loop 名 輪, ループ
- [ ] lumen 名 ルーメン（光束の単位）
- [ ] luminous 動 発光する

M
- [ ] magnify 動 拡大する
- [ ] megawatt 名 100万ワット
- [ ] modulation 名 （周波数の）変調
- [ ] motherboard 名 母板

N
- [ ] national grid 名 全国電力網
- [ ] negative 形 陰電気, 負の
- [ ] network 名 回路網
- [ ] non-polar 形 無極性の

O
- [ ] off-grid 名 グリッド遮断電圧
- [ ] optics 名 光学
- [ ] oscillate 動 発振[振動]する
- [ ] outlet 名 （電気の）差込口
- [ ] overload 動 （回路に）負荷をかけすぎる

Expand Your Vocabulary (Information Technology)

P
- [ ] patch board 名 配線板
- [ ] photocell 名 光電電池
- [ ] photoelectric 形 光電子の
- [ ] photovoltaic cell 名 光起電力電池
- [ ] piezoelectric 形 圧電の
- [ ] polarization 名 （電気の）分極化
- [ ] positron 名 陽電池, ポジトロン
- [ ] power cord 名 電気コード
- [ ] power outage 名 停電
- [ ] probe 名 （計測用の）深針, 電極プローブ
- [ ] property 名 特性, 属性
- [ ] pylon 名 （高圧線用の）鉄塔

R
- [ ] radiation 名 放射線
- [ ] receptacle 名 ソケット, コンセント
- [ ] recharge 動 （電気を）再充電する
- [ ] rechargeable 形 再充電可能な
- [ ] rectifier 名 整流器
- [ ] rectify 動 整流（交流を直流に換える）する
- [ ] relay 名 継電器
- [ ] remote 形 遠隔操作の
- [ ] repel 動 反発する
- [ ] resistivity 名 抵抗率
- [ ] resistor 名 抵抗器
- [ ] resonance 名 共振現象
- [ ] reticulation 名 網目模様
- [ ] rewire 動 （家などの）電気の配線を取り替える

S
- [ ] semiconductor 名 半導体
- [ ] spectral 形 スペクトル[分光]の
- [ ] static 形 静電の
- [ ] storage 名 （蓄電池の）蓄電

T
- [ ] thermistor 名 半導体装置, サーミスタ
- [ ] thyristor 名 半導体素子, サーリスタ

U
- [ ] unplug 動 プラグを抜く

V
- [ ] voltage 名 電圧

Z
- [ ] zapper 名 電流によって殺傷できる電気装置, 害虫駆除装置

Information Technology

A
- [ ] access provider 名 接続業者

B
- [ ] banner 名 バナー（Webページでサイト名などを表示する画像）
- [ ] bookmark 名 ブックマーク（よく見るURLを記録する機能）
- [ ] boot 名 ブート（コンピュータの）起動, 立ち上げ
- [ ] bounce 名 はね返り（配送時のエラーのためのメールの返送）

C
- [ ] cache 名 キャッシュ（コンピュータメモリに蓄積させた一時的情報）
- [ ] chain mail 名 （連鎖的に転送を繰り返させる意図を持つメール）
- [ ] checksum 名 チェックサム（誤り検出方式の一つ）
- [ ] clipboard 名 クリップボード（データの一時的格納の記憶領域）
- [ ] clone 名 クローン（他メーカー機種との互換機）
- [ ] compile 名 （プログラムを機械語に変換すること）
- [ ] configuration 名 構成, 環境設定
- [ ] connectivity 名 （他のシステムとの）接続性
- [ ] cookie 名 クッキー（Webサイトにアクセスしたユーザーの情報を記録・保存し, 次回に利用する技術）
- [ ] crash 動 （コンピュータシステムが）停止する

D
- [ ] data processing 名 データ処理, 情報処理
- [ ] decrypt 動 （暗号化されたデータを）復号する, 解読する
- [ ] default 名 初期設定, デフォルト
- [ ] dial-up 形 電話回線を利用した
- [ ] digital divide 名 情報格差
- [ ] documentation 名 文書化
- [ ] dump 動 （記憶内容を）出力する

E
- [ ] e-commerce 名 電子取引
- [ ] emoticon 名 エモーティコン（感情を表現する）顔文字
- [ ] encryption 名 暗号化
- [ ] extension 名 拡張子

F
- [ ] falsification 名 改ざん（悪意ある情報の無断変更）
- [ ] file extension 名 ファイル拡張子
- [ ] file sharing 名 ファイル共有
- [ ] flag 名 フラッグ（識別や表示のためデータにつけられる標識）
- [ ] flame 名 （電子掲示板などでの）ののしり, 攻撃的論争, 炎上
- [ ] flatscreen 名 平面パネル表示装置
- [ ] freeware 名 （無料で利用できるソフトウェア）

H
- [ ] handheld 名 （持ち運びしやすい小型の端末機）
- [ ] hot key 名 ホットキー（特定機能を直接呼び出せるキー）
- [ ] hypertext 名 （画面上から直接アクセスできる）テキスト

Expand Your Vocabulary (Environmental / Urban / Architectural Engineering)

I
- [ ] infect 動 （ウィルスなどでコンピュータが）汚染する
- [ ] infection 名 （コンピュータの）感染, 汚染
- [ ] information asset 名 （個人や組織が持つ価値ある）情報資産
- [ ] information manipulation 名 情報操作
- [ ] interface 名 インターフェース（情報をやり取りする境界部分）
- [ ] internet protocol 名 （データ通信を行うために必要な）通信規約
- [ ] intranet 名 （企業内のネットワーク）

K
- [ ] killer app 名 特長, 決めて

L
- [ ] load 動 （プログラムなどを）読み込む
- [ ] log 名 （コンピュータの利用の記録）
- [ ] log in [on] 動 コンピュータの使用を開始する

M
- [ ] malware 名 マルウェア（悪質なソフトウェアやコード）
- [ ] message board 名 （ウェブサイト上の）伝言板
- [ ] mirroring 名 （2台の補助記憶装置に同じデータを書き込むこと）
- [ ] modem 名 モデム（通信のための変復調装置）
- [ ] motherboard 名 主回路基板, マザーボード
- [ ] multimedia 名 マルチメディア（多メディアを用いた伝達方式）
- [ ] multitasking 名 多重タスク処理

N
- [ ] nethead 名 有効落差, 正味落差
- [ ] netizen 名 ネチズン（ネットワーク上の仮想市民）
- [ ] newbie 名 新参者
- [ ] newsgroup 名 （インターネット加入者で共通の関心を持つ集団）

O
- [ ] offline 名 オフライン（コンピュータがネットに接続していない）
- [ ] online 名 オンライン（主にコンピュータと接続されている）
- [ ] open-source 名 オープンソース（無料配布・無料改変プログラム）

P
- [ ] parallel port 名 （周辺機器を接続するためのインターフェース）
- [ ] patch 名 パッチ（プログラムの応急的な修正）
- [ ] personal organizer 名 電子手帳
- [ ] portal 名 ポータル（インターネットへの入り口となるサイト）
- [ ] procedure 名 プログラムの処理手続き
- [ ] protocol 名 通信規約, プロトコル

R
- [ ] reboot 名 動 再起動（する）
- [ ] rip 動 リッピング（CDやDVDからデータを吸い出す）
- [ ] router 名 ルーター（ネットワーク間の接続をする中継装置）

S
- [ ] scan 動 走査する, スキャン
- [ ] screenshot 名 画面のコピー
- [ ] simulation 名 模擬実験
- [ ] smiley 名 （文字・記号で表情を表した）顔文字
- [ ] spoofing 名 なりすまし
- [ ] streaming 名 （動画や音声データを受信しながら再生する技術）
- [ ] string 名 文字列, 一連
- [ ] stylus 名 スタイラス（ペン状の位置指示装置）
- [ ] suite 名 総合ソフトウェアパッケージ
- [ ] swipe 動 指紋をスキャンする

T
- [ ] tag 名 タグ（テキスト上に埋め込む標識情報）
- [ ] template 名 型板, テンプレート
- [ ] toggle 動 （同一の操作でON, OFFなど二つの状態を切り換えること）
- [ ] troll 動 名 （電子掲示板などで意図的に）あおる, 釣り

U
- [ ] ubiquitous 形 いたるところで
- [ ] undelete 動 復元する

V
- [ ] virtual memory 名 仮想メモリー
- [ ] voice-activated 名 音声起動録音装置

W
- [ ] web hosting 名 ホームページサービス
- [ ] webcam 名 ウェブカメラ（リアルタイムで写しているカメラ）
- [ ] weblog 名 ウェブログ（日記的に書きつづったウェブサイト）
- [ ] wild card 名 ワイルドカード（任意の文字を表す特殊文字）
- [ ] wiretapping 名 盗聴
- [ ] workstation 名 ワークステーション（マルチタスク機能, 大容量メモリなどをもつコンピュータ）

Z
- [ ] zip 名 （ウィンドウズなどで使われるデータ圧縮形式またはその拡張子）

Environmental Ⓔ/ Urban Ⓤ/ Architectural Ⓐ Engineering

A
- [ ] absorbance 名 吸光度 Ⓔ
- [ ] acid rain 名 酸性雨 Ⓔ
- [ ] activated carbon adsorption 名 活性炭吸着 Ⓔ
- [ ] activated sludge process 名 活性汚泥法 Ⓔ
- [ ] active earth pressure 名 主働土圧 Ⓤ

Expand Your Vocabulary (Environmental / Urban / Architectural Engineering)

- [ ] adsorption 名 吸着, 吸収 E
- [ ] aerosol 名 エアロゾル, 煙霧剤 E
- [ ] aggregate 名 骨材 U
- [ ] air entraining agent 名 AE減水剤 U
- [ ] alkali-aggregate reaction 名 アルカリ骨材反応 U
- [ ] alkali-silica reaction 名 アルカリシリカ反応 U
- [ ] anaerobic digestion 名 嫌気性消化 E
- [ ] application for building confirmation 名 確認申請 A
- [ ] aquifer 名 帯水層 E
- [ ] architectural design 名 建築設計[意匠] A

B
- [ ] batter board 名 遣方 A
- [ ] beam [girder, joist] 名 梁 A
- [ ] bearing capacity 名 支持力 U
- [ ] bearing wall 名 耐力壁 A
- [ ] bending moment 名 曲げモーメント U
- [ ] biochemical oxygen demand 名 生物化学的酸素要求量(BOD) E
- [ ] biodegradable 形 生物分解性の E
- [ ] biodiversity 名 生物多様性 E
- [ ] biosphere 名 生物圏 E
- [ ] buckling 名 座屈 U
- [ ] building code [regulations] 名 建築法規 A
- [ ] building frame [skeleton] 名 躯体 A

C
- [ ] carbon dioxide 名 炭酸ガス, 二酸化炭素 E
- [ ] carbon monoxide 名 一酸化炭素 E
- [ ] carcinogen 名 発がん物質 E
- [ ] catalytic converter 名 触媒コンバーター E
- [ ] centroid 名 図心 U
- [ ] chemical oxygen demand 名 化学的酸素要求量(COD) E
- [ ] chlorination 名 塩素消毒 E
- [ ] climate change 名 気候変動 E
- [ ] coagulation settling 名 凝集沈殿 E
- [ ] coarse aggregate 名 粗骨材 U
- [ ] coastal waters 名 沿岸水域 E
- [ ] coefficient of roughness 名 粗度係数 U
- [ ] commencement of work 名 着工 A
- [ ] completion 名 施工[竣工] A
- [ ] compost 名 堆肥 E
- [ ] conjugate depth 名 共役水深 U
- [ ] conservation 名 保護, 保存 E
- [ ] conservationist 名 保護主義者 E
- [ ] consolidation 名 圧密 U
- [ ] contaminate 動 汚す, 汚染する E
- [ ] contamination 名 汚染状態, 汚濁 E
- [ ] continuous beam 名 連続ばり U
- [ ] control section 名 支配断面 U
- [ ] cooling agent 名 冷却剤 E
- [ ] courtyard 名 中庭 A
- [ ] creep 名 クリープ(一定の応力でも, 物体の塑性変形が時間とともに増加する現象) U
- [ ] critical depth 名 限界水深 U
- [ ] critical slope 名 限界勾配 U
- [ ] critical velocity 名 限界流速 U
- [ ] cross section 名 断面 U

D
- [ ] daylighting design 名 採光設計 A
- [ ] deflection (angle) 名 たわみ(角) U
- [ ] deforestation 名 森林伐採, 山林開発 E
- [ ] demolition work 名 解体工事 A
- [ ] desertification 名 砂漠化 E
- [ ] destruction 名 破壊, 破滅の原因 E
- [ ] detergent 形 洗浄性の E
- [ ] diminish 動 減らす, 少なくする E
- [ ] dirt 名 ゴミ E
- [ ] disposable 形 使い捨ての E
- [ ] diversity 名 多様性 E
- [ ] drawings and specifications 名 設計図書 A
- [ ] dressing room 名 脱衣室 A
- [ ] drought 名 干ばつ, 日照り E
- [ ] dump 名 ゴミ捨て場 E
- [ ] dynamic structure 名 動的構造物 U
- [ ] dynamic water pressure 名 動水圧 U

E
- [ ] earth pressure 名 土圧 U
- [ ] earth retaining [sheathing] 名 山[土]留め A
- [ ] earthquake resistant construction 名 耐震構造 A
- [ ] eaves 名 軒 A
- [ ] ecosystem 名 生態系 E
- [ ] effective stress 名 有効応力 U
- [ ] elastic modulus 名 弾性係数 U
- [ ] emission 名 排気, 排出 E
- [ ] endangered 形 絶滅の危機に瀕した E
- [ ] endangered species 名 絶滅危惧種 E
- [ ] energy-efficient 形 省エネルギーな E
- [ ] environmentalist 名 環境保護主義者 E

Expand Your Vocabulary (Environmental / Urban / Architectural Engineering)

- equipment planning 名 設備計画 Ⓐ
- erode 動 浸食する Ⓤ
- erosion 名 浸食 Ⓤ
- exhaust fumes 名 排気ガス Ⓔ
- extinct 形 絶滅した、死に絶えた Ⓔ
- extinction 名 絶滅、死滅 Ⓔ

F
- famine 名 食料不足、飢饉 Ⓔ
- fertile 形 肥沃な Ⓔ
- fertilizer 名 化学肥料 Ⓔ
- fine aggregate 名 細骨材 Ⓤ
- fire alarm equipment 名 火災報知機 Ⓐ
- fire escape stairs 名 避難階段 Ⓐ
- (fire) hydrant 名 消火栓 Ⓐ
- fittings 名 建具 Ⓐ
- fixed bearing 名 固定端 Ⓤ
- floc 名 フロック（凝集作用によって生成した大きな粒子）Ⓔ
- footing [foundation] 名 基礎 Ⓐ
- form [mold, shuttering] 名 型枠 Ⓐ
- fossil fuel 名 化石燃料 Ⓔ
- fume 名 煙霧 Ⓤ

G
- geological survey 名 地質調査 Ⓐ
- geotechnical engineering 名 土質工学、土質力学 Ⓤ
- geothermal 形 地熱の Ⓔ
- global warming 名 地球の温暖化 Ⓔ
- gravel 名 礫 Ⓤ
- greenhouse effect 名 温室効果 Ⓔ
- groundwater 名 地下水 Ⓔ

H
- habitat 名 生息地 Ⓔ
- head loss 名 損失水頭 Ⓤ
- heat insulation property 名 断熱性能 Ⓐ
- heat wave 名 酷暑、熱波 Ⓔ
- heavy metal 名 重金属 Ⓔ
- herbicide 名 除草剤 Ⓔ
- hydraulic gradient 名 動水勾配 Ⓤ
- hydraulic jump 名 跳水 Ⓤ
- hydraulic mean depth 名 径深 Ⓤ
- hydrocarbon 名 炭化水素 Ⓔ
- hydrostatic pressure 名 静水圧 Ⓤ

I
- improvement [repair] 名 改修 Ⓐ
- indoor environment 名 室内環境 Ⓐ
- insulation 名 断熱材 Ⓐ
- internal friction angle 名 内部摩擦角 Ⓤ

L
- laminar flow 名 層流 Ⓤ
- landfill 名 埋め立てゴミ処理 Ⓔ
- landscape architecture 名 造園 Ⓐ
- landslide 名 地すべり Ⓤ
- liquefaction 名 液状化 Ⓤ

M
- marking 名 墨出し Ⓐ
- membrane filtration 名 膜ろ過 Ⓔ
- methane 名 メタン、沼気 Ⓔ
- microfiltration 名 精密ろ過法 Ⓔ
- moment of inertia of area 名 断面2次モーメント Ⓤ

N
- nano-filtration 名 ナノろ過法 Ⓔ
- neutral axis 名 中立軸 Ⓤ

O
- oil slick 名 （水面上の）油膜 Ⓔ
- organic 形 有機肥料を用いた Ⓔ
- overfertilization 名 肥料のやりすぎ Ⓔ
- ozonation 名 オゾン処理 Ⓔ
- ozone layer 名 オゾン層 Ⓔ

P
- partition wall 名 間仕切壁 Ⓐ
- permanganate consumption 名 過マンガン酸消費量 Ⓔ
- permeability 名 透水性 Ⓤ
- pesticide 名 殺虫剤、害虫駆除剤 Ⓔ
- petroleum 名 石油 Ⓔ
- physiognomy of a house 名 家相 Ⓐ
- piling [pile driving] 名 杭打ち Ⓐ
- pin bearing 名 ピン支承 Ⓤ
- plasticity 名 塑性 Ⓤ
- plot [lot, site] 名 敷地 Ⓐ
- poisonous 形 有毒な Ⓔ
- pollutant 名 汚染物質 Ⓔ
- pollution 名 公害 Ⓔ
- precipitation 名 降水量 Ⓔ
- preservation 名 保護、維持 Ⓔ
- prevention 名 防止、予防 Ⓔ
- programming [project] 名 企画 Ⓐ
- progress schedule 名 工程表 Ⓐ

R
- rainforest 名 熱帯雨林 Ⓔ
- rapid sand filtration 名 急速ろ過 Ⓔ
- registered architect of the first class 名 一級建築士 Ⓐ
- reinforced concrete 名 鉄筋コンクリート Ⓐ
- reinforcement [reinforcing bar] 名 鉄筋 Ⓐ
- remedial 形 救済的な、改善的な Ⓔ
- renewable 形 再生可能な、継続できる Ⓔ
- reusable 形 再利用できる Ⓔ
- reverse osmosis

Expand Your Vocabulary (Environmental / Urban / Architectural Engineering)

- 名 逆浸透法 Ⓔ
- ☐ rigid frame structure
  - 名 ラーメン構造（柱と梁を一体化した構造）Ⓐ
- ☐ roller bearing
  - 名 ローラー支承 Ⓤ
- ☐ roof light window 名 天窓 Ⓐ
- ☐ roof planting 名 屋上緑化 Ⓔ

S

- ☐ scaffold(ing) 名 足場 Ⓐ
- ☐ seismically isolated structure
  - 名 免震構造 Ⓐ
- ☐ sewage plant
  - 名 下水処理場 Ⓔ
- ☐ sewage works
  - 名 下水道事業 Ⓔ
- ☐ sewer 名 下水道 Ⓔ
- ☐ shear 名 剪断 Ⓤ
- ☐ shear stress 名 剪断応力 Ⓤ
- ☐ silt 名 沈泥, シルト Ⓤ
- ☐ slab 名 厚板, スラブ Ⓐ
- ☐ slope failure 名 斜面崩壊 Ⓤ
- ☐ sludge 名 汚物, ヘドロ Ⓔ
- ☐ smoke compartment
  - 名 防煙区画 Ⓐ
- ☐ soil compaction 名 締固め Ⓤ
- ☐ solvent 形 溶解力がある Ⓐ
- ☐ sorption 名 吸着 Ⓔ
- ☐ sound insulation 名 遮音 Ⓐ
- ☐ specific energy
  - 名 比エネルギ Ⓤ
- ☐ starvation 名 飢餓 Ⓔ
- ☐ static structure
  - 名 静定構造物 Ⓤ
- ☐ steady flow 名 定常流 Ⓤ
- ☐ steel encased reinforced concrete 名 鉄骨鉄筋コンクリート構造 Ⓐ
- ☐ steel structure 名 鉄骨構造 Ⓐ
- ☐ strain 名 ひずみ Ⓤ
- ☐ stratosphere 名 成層圏 Ⓔ
- ☐ stress 名 応力 Ⓤ
- ☐ structural mechanics
  - 名 構造力学 Ⓤ
- ☐ subcritical flow 名 常流 Ⓤ
- ☐ supercritical flow 名 射流 Ⓤ
- ☐ suspended solids
  - 名 浮遊物質 (SS) Ⓤ
- ☐ sustainable 形 持続可能な Ⓔ

T

- ☐ timber structure 名 木造 Ⓐ
- ☐ titration 名 滴定 Ⓔ
- ☐ total organic carbon
  - 名 全有機炭素 (TOC) Ⓔ
- ☐ total stress 名 全応力 Ⓤ
- ☐ toxic 形 有毒な Ⓔ
- ☐ toxic waste 名 有害廃棄物 Ⓔ
- ☐ turbidity 名 濁度 Ⓔ
- ☐ turbulent flow 名 乱流 Ⓤ
- ☐ two-way escape
  - 名 二方向避難 Ⓐ

U

- ☐ ultrafiltration 名 限外ろ過法 Ⓔ
- ☐ uniform flow 名 等流 Ⓤ
- ☐ unleaded petrol 名 （鉛化合物で処理されなかった）ガソリン Ⓔ
- ☐ urban sprawl 名 都市乱開発 Ⓔ
- ☐ urbanization 名 都会化 Ⓔ

V

- ☐ vegitation 名 植被 Ⓔ
- ☐ ventilation 名 換気 Ⓐ

W

- ☐ wall construction
  - 名 壁式構造 Ⓐ
- ☐ waste water 名 廃水 Ⓔ
- ☐ water head 名 水頭 Ⓤ
- ☐ water works 名 水道事業 Ⓔ
- ☐ wetland 名 湿地, 湿原 Ⓔ
- ☐ wetted perimeter 名 潤辺 Ⓤ
- ☐ windpark 名 （電気を起こすのに風力タービンを使用する）発電所 Ⓔ

Z

- ☐ zoning 名 （土地計画による）地区制, 用途地域分け Ⓔ

Acknowledgement

Science Lab Ⓐ, Ⓑの4つの実験は，すべて日本ガイシ株式会社『NGK サイエンスサイト』の記事を基に編集してあります。この実験に関するすべての権利は，日本ガイシ株式会社にあります。

クリエーティブディレクション	塚本良介（株式会社日本経済社）
アートディレクション	冨士義継（株式会社 OAD）
デザイン	塚原真二（株式会社 OAD）　深見浩嗣（株式会社 OAD）
	宮下歩（株式会社 OAD）
プロデュース	内田陽子（日本ガイシ株式会社）
コピー	大西光（オフィスオーツー）
写真	水川敏治（オフィス水川）
イラスト	坂倉直道（株式会社 OAD）
監修	滝川洋二（東海大学特任教授）

引用文献

■ **UNIT 1**
Excerpted from *Science Made Easy* © 2007 Dorling Kindersley Ltd.Used with Permission.

■ **UNIT 2**
DENSO WAVE, QR Code.com: History of QR Code
http://www.qrcode.com/en/history/

■ **UNIT 3**
Hal Iggulden and Conn Iggulden, *The DANGEROUS Book for Boys*. HarperCollins ©2007.

■ **UNIT 5**
Desmond Morris, *MANWATCHING: A Field Guide to Human Behaviour*. Jonathan Cape Ltd. 1977.

■ **UNIT 6**
Ajith Kumar J., Amaresh Chakrabarti, 'Bounded awareness and tacit knowledge: revisiting Challenger disaster'. *Journal of knowledge Management*. Emerald Group Publishing, 2012.

■ **UNIT 7**
'It's official! Element 113 was discovered at RIKEN', 2015.12.31.
'Lucky number 113: The creation of an atom with 113 protons adds a new element to the periodic table', 2016.01.05.
'IUPAC begins Public Review of nihonium and Nh, the proposed name and symbol for the new element 113', 2016.06.08.

■ **UNIT 8**
Lisa Randall, 'Chapter fifteen TRUTH, BEAUTY, AND OTHER SCIENTIFIC MISCONCEPTIONS' *KNOCKING ON THE HEAVEN'S DOOR*. London: Vintage, 2012.
From the presentation by Murray Gell-Mann on Beauty, Truth and … Physics in TED Conference in March, 2007.

写真・図版提供

■ **UNIT 1**
shutterstock/ユニオンプラン

■ **UNIT 2**
PIXTA/有限会社原田青果

■ **UNIT 3**
shutterstock/ユニオンプラン

■ **UNIT 4**
アフロ/PIXTA/shutterstock

■ **UNIT 5**
PIXTA/ユニオンプラン

■ **UNIT 6**
アフロ/shutterstock

■ **UNIT 7**
アフロ/理化学研究所

■ **UNIT 8**
アフロ/shutterstock

■ UNIT 4

Cynthia, Breazeal. *Emotion and social humanoid robots*: MIT USA, 2002.

Dr. Sally, Ward. *Baby Talk*. arrow books. UK, 2004.

Babies are specially attuned to our voices and emotions, Science Daily. 2011.

　　http://www.sciencedaily.com/releases/2011/06/110630122003.htm/

Hegel Frank et al. *Understanding social robots*: Bielefeld University, 2009.

BBC NEWS ASIA, 4 August 2013

　　http://www.bbc.com/news/world-asia-23565121/

TIME, June 8 2014

　　http://time.com/2845040/robot-emotions-pepper-softbank/

P. Brown, S.C. Levinson, *Politeness: Some Universals in Language Usage*: Cambridge University Press, 1987.

石黒 浩.『どうすれば「人」を創れるか―アンドロイドになった私―』新潮文庫.2011

Tony, Buzan. *The mind map book: Unlock your creativity, Boost your memory, Change your life*. Pearson Education Ltd, 2010.

関山 健治.『英語での「慰め」表現にみられる母語からの語用論的転移―日本人英語学習者の場合―』 *Pragmatic Transfer in Consolation: A Case in Japanese EFL Learners*.1999.

　　http://sekky.tripod.com/

■ UNIT 5

Story from BBC NEWS:

　　http://news.bbc.co.uk/go/pr/fr/-/2/hi/uk_news/england/bristol/somerset/7459915.stm/

■ UNIT 6

http://ethics.tamu.edu/Portals/3/Case%20Studies/Shuttle.pdf/

The Space Shuttle Challenger Disaster. Department of Philosophy and Department of Mechanical Engineering. Texas A&M University. NSF Grant NumberDIR-9012252.

■ UNIT 7

http://www.nishina.riken.jp/research/113_e.html/

■著作者
代表　奥村信彦　　国立長野工業高等専門学校
主査　奥山慶洋　　白鷗大学教育学部

乙黒麻記子　日本大学理工学部　　　　　　　　小野雄一　筑波大学グローバルコミュニケーション教育センター
中川洋子　　駿河台大学グローバル教育センター　本田謙介　国立茨城工業高等専門学校
吉村理英　　国立小山工業高等専門学校　　　　開隆堂出版株式会社編集部

■英文校閲
ジョージ・マクレーン　琉球大学　　　　　　　ウィリアム・ロジスキー　山梨学院大学

■実験監修
滝川洋二　ガリレオ工房理事長（東海大学特任教授）

■編集協力
井腰松夫　佐野日本大学中等教育学校　　　　　大内栄子　東洋大学文学部
岡田　晃　国立小山工業高等専門学校　　　　　金﨑八重　大阪府立大学工業高等専門学校
清水義彦　富山県立大学工学部　　　　　　　　山村啓人　国立富山高等専門学校
楽山　進　国立富山高等専門学校

■表紙・本文デザイン
タクトシステム株式会社

平成29年 3月 6日　初版発行
平成31年 1月21日　3版発行

著作者　奥村信彦　ほか7名（別記）
発　行　開隆堂出版株式会社　代表者　大熊隆晴
　　　　〒113-8608　東京都文京区向丘1丁目13番1号
　　　　電話／東京（03）5684-6115（編集）
発　売　開隆館出版販売株式会社
　　　　〒113-8608　東京都文京区向丘1丁目13番1号
　　　　電話／東京（03）5684-6118（販売）
印　刷　壮光舎印刷株式会社

◎本書を無断で転載，複製することを禁ずる。
◎本書に関する指導書・自習書・練習書，およびこれに類するものを無断で発行することを禁ずる。